The Central Pacific Campaign, 1943-1944: A Bibliography

Meckler's Bibliographies of Battles and Leaders

Series Editor: Myron J. Smith, Jr.
Series ISBN 0-88736-517-5

1. The Battle of Antietam and the Maryland Campaign of 1862: A Bibliography
   D. Scott Hartwig
   ISBN 0-88736-321-0   CIP   1990

2. The Central Pacific Campaign, 1943 - 1944: A Bibliography
   James T. Controvich
   ISBN 0-88736-325-3   CIP   1990

3. American Warplanes 1908 - 1988: A Bibliography
   Myron J. Smith, Jr.
   ISBN 0-88736-383-0   CIP   1990

4. The Battle of Pearl Harbor: A Bibliography
   Myron J. Smith, Jr.
   ISBN 0-88736-305-9   CIP   1990

5. The Battles of Coral Sea and Midway, May - June 1942: A Bibliography
   Myron J. Smith, Jr.
   ISBN 0-88736-683-X   CIP   *forthcoming*

6. Julius Caesar: A Bibliography
   Diane R. Gordon
   ISBN 0-88736-693-7   CIP   *forthcoming*

7. The Battle of Jutland: A Bibliography
   Eugene Rasor
   ISBN 0-88736-669-4   CIP   *forthcoming*

8. The Falklands/Malvinas Conflict: A Bibliography
   Eugene Rasor
   ISBN 0-88736-668-6   CIP   *forthcoming*

9. The Normandy Invasion, 1944: A Bibliography
   Colin F. Baxter
   ISBN 0-88736-557-4   CIP   *forthcoming*

10. Military Fortifications: A Bibliography
    Dale E. Floyd
    ISBN 0-88736-307-5   CIP   *forthcoming*

11. The War of Spanish Succession: A Bibliography
    W. Calvin Dickinson
    ISBN 0-88736-694-5   CIP   *forthcoming*

The Central Pacific Campaign, 1943-1944: A Bibliography

James T. Controvich

Meckler
Westport • London

Library of Congress Cataloging-in-Publication Data

Controvich, James T.
   The central Pacific campaign, 1943 - 1944 : a bibliography / by James T. Controvich.
     p. cm. -- (Meckler's bibliographies of battles and leaders ; 2)
   Includes bibliographical references.
   ISBN 0-88736-325-3 (alk. paper) : $
   1. World War, 1939-1945--Campaigns--Pacific Ocean--Bibliography.
2. World War, 1939-1945--Oceania--Bibliography. 3. United States-
Armed Forces--History--World War, 1939-1945--Bibliography.
4. Pacific Area--History--20th century--Bibliography. I. Title.
II. Series.
Z6207.W8C66   1990
[D767.9]
016.94054'26--dc20   90-5508
                                                                                      CIP

British Library Cataloguing in Publication Data

Controvich, James T.
   The Central Pacific campaign, 1943-1944 : a
   bibliography. - (Meckler's bibliographies of battles and leaders; v. 2).
   1. World War 2. Pacific campaigns - Bibliographies
   I. Title
   016.9405426

ISBN 0-88736-325-3

Copyright © 1990 Meckler Corporation. All rights reserved. No part of this publication may be reproduced in any form by any means without prior written permission from the publisher, except by a reviewer who may quote brief passages in review.

Meckler Corporation, 11 Ferry Lane West, Westport, CT 06880.
Meckler Ltd., Grosvenor Gardens House, Grosvenor Gardens,
   London SW1W 0BS, U.K.

Printed on acid free paper.
Printed and bound in the United States of America.

Contents

Series Editor's Foreword vii

1. Campaign Narrative 1
2. General Reference Works 11
   Atlases 11
   Bibliographies 12
   Research Aids 15
   Newspaper Indices 17
3. General Histories 19
   General Titles 19
   Air Operations 37
   Naval Operations 43
4. Memoirs and Biographies 53
5. Gilbert Islands Operations 63
   General Works 63
6. Marshall Islands Operations 71
   General Works 71
   Eniwetok Atoll 74
   Kwajalein Atoll 74
   Majuro 75
   Makin 75
   Roi-Namur 76
7. Marianas Islands Operations 77
   General Works 77
   Air Operations 78
   Naval Operations 79
   Saipan 80
   Tinian 83
   Guam 83
8. Army Air Force Unit Histories 87
9. Army Unit Histories 97
10. Marine Corps Unit Histories 107
11. Naval Unit Histories 113

Index of Authors and Names 143

Series Editor's Foreword

In *The Central Pacific Campaign*, James Controvich has compiled a timely guide to the literature surrounding some of America's most famous World War II amphibious operations. Significant for its military aspects, including the fights at Tarawa, Saipan, Tinian, and Guam, and its strategic ramifications, most importantly in the provision of a launching pad for the B-29 air campaign against the Japanese home islands, the Central Pacific Campaign, a uniquely and almost 100% American effort devoid of Allied assistance, continues to attract widespread interest.

The scope of this work is comprehensive. The author cites books, memoirs, monographs, periodical/journal articles, documents, theses and dissertations, and unit histories, the latter a subclass of military literature in the control of which Controvich has been acclaimed. Not only has he provided us with ample references on the campaign itself, but his attention to and inclusion of a heavy dose of unit information should prove invaluable.

With such a variety of studies from which to selelct one or more specific or general topics or subtopics — along with a convenient campaign history and detailed index — the reader can quickly locate the most potentially pertinent or available material on these decidedly important military clashes. Controvich's study is the most detailed bibliography ever prepared on his topic; students, researchers, historians, museum personnel, teachers and librarians — to say nothing of World War II buffs — will benefit from this valuable reference work. I am delighted to see this title's inclusion in Meckler's series of *Bibliographies of Battles and Leaders* and commend it to you.

Myron J. Smith, Jr.
Salem, West Virginia

1.
Campaign Narrative

By January of 1943, the general public of the Allied Powers were beginning to read increasingly favorable news from the various fronts. The American and Allied forces were advancing in Sicily, the Russians were counterattacking along their front, the American Marine and Army units were advancing across Guadalcanal. News to the Japanese public was still being presented with an optimistic view. The Japanese had been at war with China since 1931, and although there had been setbacks at Guadalcanal, New Guinea, in the Coral Sea, and at Midway, the war had not yet taken a dramatic shift in the balance of power.

Also in January, Allied leadership met in Casablanca and the decision was made to allow the Americans to continue on with their offensive after Guadalcanal to keep the Japanese off balance. The Conference agreement targeted the breakthrough of the Bismarck Islands Barrier, and advocated that the Americans retain the initiative. The American strategists were struggling with which approach to Japan should be given priority, the drive through the Philippines which had a strong moral and political backing or through the Central Pacific which was the most direct route to Japan. The debate continued as increasing amounts of weapons and troops were arriving.

The Navy, in particular, was just beginning to benefit from the impact of construction programs that were on the drawing boards only two years earlier. The "Essex" class fleet carriers, which would form

2 THE CENTRAL PACIFIC CAMPAIGN, 1943-1944

the nucleus of the fast carrier task forces, were just beginning to arrive. Escorts, battleships, auxiliaries were also arriving in increasingly larger numbers. By June of 1943, new ship reinforcements in the Pacific amounted to 12 fleet and light carriers, 6 fast battleships, and many cruisers and escorts. More important, the construction tempo in the shipyards and factories would triple the latter numbers in less than a year. The Japanese on the other hand, had not been able replace combat losses, much less add to their fleet. By early 1943, the Japanese were able to replace only 5 carriers, these being for the most part conversions from merchantmen hulls. For the Japanese the war of attrition was being lost.

In May of 1943, the American Joint Chiefs of Staff adopted a strategic plan for the defeat of Japan. Included in it was the capture of the Gilbert, Marshall, and Caroline Islands. American strategy still envisioned the landing on the coast of China to seal off the sea transportation routes to Japan and to provide a staging area for the ultimate invasion of the Japanese mainland.

The seizure of the Gilberts, formerly a British Colony before being occupied by the Japanese in 1941, was considered a prerequisite for the capture of the Marshall Islands. It was decided to seize Tarawa and Makin (Butarutari) Atolls in order to provide air bases to permit land based aircraft to support the Marshalls operations. The date established for the Gilberts operation, codenamed "Galvanic", was late October or early November 1943. The overall command would be under Admiral Chester Nimitz, with Admiral Raymond Spruance commanding the Fifth Fleet as the tactical commander. The amphibious forces would be under Admiral R. Kelly Turner, also known as "Terrible Turner", and the ground Marine units under the command of Major General Holland M. Smith, USMC, nicknamed "Howlin´ Mad Smith". This team would eventually command all the major assaults in the Central Pacific.

Intelligence indicated that Makin was lightly garrisoned and the 27th Infantry Division was assigned to capture it. The 27th was an Army National Guard unit from New York, commanded by Major General Ralph C. Smith. Betio or as it became to be known, Tarawa, was a much different picture, the Japanese were estimated to be in excess of 4,500 combat troops under the command of Admiral Meichi Shibasaki, IJN, supported by artillery up to eight inches in size. Artillery and troops were protected in bomb proof shelters reinforced with sand, concrete, and steel. Information concerning the island tides was almost non-existent. Planners were relying on tidal hydrographic charts and information that were almost a century old. The assault troops would pay dearly for the lack of accurate information.

The assault of Tarawa started on the morning of November 21, after two hours of naval bombardment, with troops from the 2nd Marine

Division, veterans of Guadalcanal, under the command of MG Julian C. Smith, USMC. The effect of naval gunfire was greatly overestimated, particularly against underground targets. The older battleships, especially the USS Mississippi, which was serving as the flagship, was prone to lose its communications after firing its main battery of 14 inch guns. Assault tactics were yet to be fully defined as new weapons and equipment were used for the first time. Problems with the assault time tables allowed the Japanese protected in underground bunkers to man light weapons and attempt to repulse the invaders. The lack of accurate tidal information came to haunt the assault forces as Marines were forced to disembark from their landing craft over 400 yards from the beach. Japanese small arms fire inflicted a heavy toll as the Marines moved slowly toward the beach. By the evening of November 21st, Marines had only advanced 300 yards beyond the beach. Although the naval bombardment did little damage to underground troops, Japanese communications and surface installations were severely damaged. As a result Admiral Shibasaki was never able to effectively organize a coordinated counterattack on the exposed Marine positions either the first or second nights. Reinforcements permitted the Marine beachhead to bisect the island and capture the landing strip on the second day. By November 23rd, the third day, General Smith was able to announce that the island was secured and that organized resistance was ended. The Japanese garrison was literally wiped out, only few surrendered or were captured alive. American losses were just over 3,000.

With the Gilberts in Nimitz's possession permitting land based aircraft to reach the Marshalls, Central Pacific leadership began preparations for the invasion of the Marshalls which were approximatley 400 miles to the northwest. The lessons of the Gilberts were incorporated into the planning process. Debate was still ongoing regarding the direction and amount of forces that should be allotted to the Pacific commanders and who should get those forces. Military planners in Washington were visualizing two mutually supporting drives, Nimitz advancing through the Central Pacific, and MacArthur via the Southwest Pacific and the Philippines. The impact of airpower was increasingly becoming the dominant element in the planning process. The carrier task forces were permitting a much larger degree of flexibility in carrying the war to Japan and its island outposts.

American strategy in the beginning of 1944 still visualized the need to invade the Japanese mainland, accomplished by moving through the Marshalls, on to the Carolines, then to the China coast. Each step was viewed as a spring board to the next and permitted land based aircraft to support each phase. The B-29 capabilities were beginning to figure in the debate over which direction to take in the Pacific. Given the range of the aircraft, it could reach the Japanese mainland, from bases in the Marianas Islands. Army Air Force and Marine-Naval leadership in both the Central Pacific and Washington were beginning to advocate for the Central Pacific approach as the primary route in the attack on Japan.

4   THE CENTRAL PACIFIC CAMPAIGN, 1943-1944

The Marshalls operation, codenamed "Flintlock", targeted three major atolls, Majuro, Kwajalein, and Eniwetok. These islands had been in Japanese possession since 1920, and due to Japanese travel restrictions little was known about them. Operations started on January 31, 1944, with the occupation of Majuro by troops of the 106th Infantry Regiment. The Majuro Atoll was situated in the center of the Marshall Islands group, a location that was immediately capitalized on by initiating the construction of air and naval bases.

Kwajalein Atoll was comprised of two primary islands, Roi-Namur in the north, and Kwajalein to the south. Japanese forces were commanded by Rear Admiral Monzo Akiyama, IJN, with nearly 8,000 Japanese troops of all categories were targeted for two days of intensive naval and air bombardments. The lessons of Tarawa were incorporated into every facet of the operation. The operations envisioned two distinct phases; the first, the capture of Kwajalein Atoll, and later, the capture of Eniwetok Atoll. Troops of the 4th Marine Division commanded by MG Harry Schmidt, USMC, along with troops of the 7th Infantry Division veterans of the Aleutian Campaign, commanded by MG Charles H. Corlett were assigned to the assaulting forces. The Roi-Namur Island was targeted to secure an artillery platform for the assault on Kwajalein. Opposition on the Namur part of the island was slight, and it was secured by troops of the 24th Marine Regiment, on February 2nd, approximately 24 hours after the troops had landed, with over half of the Marine casualties coming from an exploding ammunition dump in a blockhouse. Army troops from the 32nd and 184th Infantry Regiments which landed on Kwajalein on February 1st, encountered more fortifications and resistance, and it was not deemed secured until February 5.

Captured documents found on Kwajalein revealed a much larger garrison on Eniwetok Atoll than originally thought. The atoll which was 375 miles northwest of Kwajalein had three primary islands; Engebi, Parry, and Eniwetok. The documents indicated that over 3,500 Japanese, principally the 1st Amphibious Brigade commanded by MG Yoshima Nishida, IJA, were located on the atoll. The rapid pace of the American forces had prevented the Japanese from constructing much more than foxholes and trenches as most of the Japanese troops had only been on the island less than a month and half before the Americans landed.

The assault of Eniwetok Atoll started early morning on February 17th with the occupation of Canna and Camellia Islands. These islands following earlier American assault techniques, began artillery platforms for both Army and Marine artillery units. Troops from the 22nd Marine Regiment landed on Engebi Island and encountered only sporadic resistance. The island was secured by early evening. On the 18th the assault of Eniwetok Atoll was initiated by troops of the 22nd

Marine and 106th Infantry Regiment. It was deemed to be secured by the 21st. The major island to secure in the atoll was Parry, the location of MG Nashida's headquarters. Elements of the 22nd Marine Regiment accomplished its seizure on February 22nd.

The ease by which the Marshalls were seized was a tribute to the incorporation of the lessons of Tarawa, and the increasing margin of forces and equipment the Americans could concentrate at will. The operations in the Marshalls were completed with less than 3,000 Marine and Army casualties. With the Marshalls in their possession, Japanese positions in the Caroline Islands became precarious. The great Japanese naval base at Truk was effectively isolated.

Planners for the Central Pacific and Southwest Areas met in Washington to discuss the future direction for operations in the Pacific. Agreement was reached with Nimitz's forces being assigned to take the Marianas Islands, and MacArthur's forces Mindanao Island in the Philippines. The Joint Chiefs of Staff were still committed to the dual approach to reaching Japan, both to keep the Japanese off balance and to take advantage of the mix of forces that were available in the Pacific. Also it was agree to by-pass the Caroline Islands, thus avoiding the large garrisons on many of the islands.

The Marianas Islands had been in Japanese possession since the First World War, before which they were a German possession. The primary targets within the Marianas Islands would be Saipan, Tinian, and Guam, an American possession since the Spanish-American War. Saipan was only 1,200 miles south of Tokyo, well within operating range of the new B-29 heavy bomber. Unlike earlier Central Pacific targets these islands would be larger and would afford the opportunity for maneuver once the forces had landed, thus requiring a larger number of forces to be involved. Another major difference from earlier operations would be the importance that the Japanese attached to these islands. The Marianas were the first group that would be within Japan's inner defense perimeter, and as such would be allotted critical forces to defend them.

Although the Japanese placed critical importance on the Marianas, they surprisingly did not until the spring of 1944, believe that they would have to defend them from assault. The rapid succession of assaults and defeats in the Gilberts, and Marshall islands caught the Japanese completely by surprise. The results of which meant that until 1944 very little effort had been made either to garrison or fortify the islands. The Japanese forces came under the overall command of Vice Admiral Chuichi, IJN, with the 31st Army commanded by Lt. General Hideyoshi Obata, responsible for the land defenses. Both had their headquarters located on Saipan. The principal army units comprising the garrison on Saipan were the 43rd Division, commanded by Lt. General Yoshitsugu Saito, and the 47th Independent Mixed

6   THE CENTRAL PACIFIC CAMPAIGN, 1943-1944

Brigade. The Japanese were hindered in their efforts to ship troops and supplies to the garrisons by American submarines as convoys attempting to reach the islands were decimated time after time. At the time of the assaults, the Japanese had 31,629 military and naval personnel on Saipan.

The American preparations for the invasion of the islands began on March 12, 1944, with the decision by the Joint Chiefs of Staff to target the islands for assault with a tentative date of June 15, 1944. Admiral Nimitz's forces by now had gained valuable experience in the assaults of the Gilberts and Marshalls, initiated the planning for "Operation Forager", the seizure of the southern islands, Saipan, Tinian, and Guam. Guam was to be the first American territory recaptured in the Central Pacific.

The assault of the islands would be divided into two phases. The northern groups of islands which includes Saipan and Tinian would be seized by troops of the V Amphibious Corps, commanded by Lt. General Holland M. Smith, USMC, and the southern island of Guam would be assaulted by troops of the III Amphibious Corps under the command of Major General Roy S. Geiger, USMC. The Northern Attack Group forces would be comprised of the 2nd and 4th Marine Divisions, 3rd Marine Division and 1st Provisional Marine Brigade making up the Southern Attack Group. A floating reserve consisting of the 27th Infantry Division and a general reserve comprised of the 77th Infantry Division. In total over 127,000 troops were assigned to the operation.

The American naval forces assigned to the operation reflected the immense industrial capacity of the United States, over 535 ships of all types including 15 fleet and light carriers, 13 new and old battleships were involved. The Japanese available fleet units included 9 fleet and light carriers, and 5 battleships.

The actual assault of Saipan, an island 18 miles long by 9 miles wide, began on the morning of June 15th, after two weeks of air and naval bombardment. The naval bombardment force under the command of Rear Admiral Jesse B. Oldendorf started on June 13th with eight battleships, many of which were salvaged from Pearl Harbor, pounding pre-selected targets. Marines from the 2nd and 4th Marine Division assault troops came under fire from Japanese artillery even before hitting the beaches. By 8:43 AM the first troops were ashore. Strong resistance was encountered and the advance was slower than anticipated. By darkness on D-Day, the Marines had only advanced to a maximum beachhead of 1,300 yards, about half the planned amount. Japanese reaction to the invasion was intense on the island and triggered a major Japanese fleet reaction, codenamed "AGO", which was intended to bring about a decisive fleet engagement with the American fleet. American picket submarines reported the Japanese fleet movements toward the Marianas, and immediately began to take a toll on them.

On the morning of June 16th, Admiral Sprunce reacting to the Japanese fleet movement reports, ordered all unnecessary ships away from the beachhead and the fast carrier task forces to form and make plans to intercept the oncoming Japanese fleet units. Only vital supplies would be allowed to unload while the opposing fleets moved toward each other. The beachhead was deemed secured by the 17th, and reinforcements continued to land. The 165th Infantry Regiment of the 27th Infantry Division landed during the night of the 17th, as the Marines expanded the beachhead to include most of the southern part of the island.

By the evening of the 17th, the Japanese fleet under the command of Vice Admiral Isaburo Ozawa, had information as to the location and strength of Sprunce's carrier task forces. Capitalizing on the superior range of the Japanese carrier aircraft, he initiated a complex maneuver to attack the American carriers. A series of four separate air attacks were launched against the Americans. In what has become known as the "Marianas Turkey Shoot" and the greatest air battle in the Pacific War, American carrier air units decimated the Japanese attackers. Only 100 of nearly 400 Japanese aircraft survived being shot down by the combat air patrol or antiaircraft fire from the American fleet. To add to the Japanese pilots' dilemma, American submarines sank two of their carriers while they were gone. After establishing the location of the Japanese carrier units, Admiral Marc Mitscher ordered an attack late in the afternoon which resulted in the sinking of another Japanese carrier and heavy damage to three others. American aircraft returned to their carriers after sunset and a number of aircraft were lost due to running out of fuel because of the extreme range of the attack and from becoming disoriented in the darkness. Although the Americans had won a resounding victory over the Japanese fleet, disappointment was strong to the fact that a number of Japanese carriers had escaped. This naval action, the Battle of the Philippine Sea, eliminated Japanese carrier aviation as a threat for the duration of the war. The imbalance between the numbers, training, and equipment would continue to become wider as the war progressed.

The troops on Saipan continued to grind on and by morning of June 22nd, troops of the 2nd and 4th Marine, and the 27th Infantry Divisions had formed a line across the island. On the morning of the 23rd, the line was ordered to begin the attack north, with the 27th Infantry Division between the two Marine divisions. The Marine units jumped off on time and made progress against the Japanese positions. The 27th Division, due to a number of complications and poor leadership, was late in jumping off and encountered more difficult terrain and resistance. By the evening LtGen. Holland M. Smith's patience with the National Guard troops of the 27th Infantry Division was exhausted, and

8   THE CENTRAL PACIFIC CAMPAIGN, 1943-1944

he relieved its commander Major General Ralph C. Smith of command of his division. It was a controversial decision and still stirs emotions to the present. By July 9th Saipan was deemed secured at a cost of 14,000 American and 42,000 Japanese (including 12,000 civilians who chose suicide rather than surrender) casualties.

No sooner had Saipan been deemed secure, when the American commanders began to plan the assault of Tinian, located only three miles to the south of Saipan. The assault began on July 24th over a very narrow beachhead on the northwest corner of the island. Troops of the 25th Marine Regiment landed on less than 200 yards of beach, obtaining a complete tactical surprise, and by the afternoon the entire regiment was ashore. Supported by massive land and sea based artillery, as well as land and carrier based air units, 2nd and 4th Marine Division units overran the island by August 2nd. American casualties amounted to approximately 2,200, compared to Japanese losses of over 5,000. The assault of Tinian in the words of LtGen. Smith was "the perfect amphibious invasion."

The recapture of Guam was the final phase of the Marianas operations. It had been postponed due to the heavy resistance encountered on Saipan and the Battle of the Philippine Sea. The primary Japanese unit on the island was the 29th Infantry Division, commanded by Lt. General Takeshi Takashina. Lt. General Hideyoshi Obata, commander of the 31st Army, who was enroute to Saipan, from a visit from Palau Island, was stranded on Guam, when the Americans landed on Saipan. Although the Japanese were more successful in providing troops and materiel to Guam, the Americans were for the first time in the Central Pacific invading an island for which they had intimate knowledge of the island and waters surrounding it.

The III Amphibious Corps was assigned the seizure of the island, it was comprised of the 3rd Marine Division, the 77th Infantry Division provided from the general reserve, and the 1st Marine Provisional Brigade. In contrast to the events on Saipan, relations between the Army and Marine units and commanders on Guam were cordial. The invasion began on July 21st with troops of the 3rd Marine Division landing on the northern beaches and troops of the 1st Provisional Brigade and 305th Infantry Regiment on the southern beaches. Both encountered strong resistance as they moved inland. By August 10th the island was deemed secured, although stragglers would continue to surrender for the next thirty years. Casualties were heavy for the Americans, over 7,000 and for the Japanese over 10,500.

The completion of the Marianas operations marked a new stage in the war in the Pacific: for the first time, Allied forces would be able to mount sustained air attacks against the Japanese homeland from bases that could easily be supplied. The fall of the Marianas and the defeat of the Japanese naval forces triggered the collapse of the Tojo government. To many Japanese, it was the real beginning of the end. Within months B-29 heavy bombers were operating from its bases and had started upon the strategic bombing campaign which would begin to level every Japanese city within range. Eventually, the aircraft carrying the first atomic bombs were launched from air fields located on Saipan.

The significance of the Central Pacific Campaign was immense. In just over fifteen months American forces advanced over 3,000 miles toward Japan, a distance comparable to Boston to Berlin. American casualties amounted to 29,000, a figure comparable to Gothic Line Campaign in Italy which lasted six months and advanced 100 miles. The American presence in the Pacific capitalized on the mobility of its forces to concentrate immense power on selected targets and by-passed and neutralized large Japanese garrisons. It provided a location for the strategic air campaign by the B-29s against the Japanese homeland and a platform for the invasion of Okinawa while securing MacArthur's eastern flank during his campaign in the Philippines. It was a uniquely American campaign with practically no allied participation and essentially a naval air campaign combined with incredibly intense and violent assaults on islands.

2.
General Reference Works

ATLASES

1. Bartholomew, John, editor. "The Times" Atlas of the World, Mid-Century Edition. London: Times Pub. Co., 1955-1959. 4 vols.
Considered one of the best atlases available.

2. Brown, Ernest F. The War in Maps: An Atlas of the New York Times Maps. New York: Oxford Univ. Press, 1946. 197 pp.
Compilation of maps taken from news articles.

3. Esposito, Vincent J. The West Point Atlas of American Wars. New York: Praeger, 1959. 2 vols.   PCarlMH
An outstanding collection of annotated maps and summaries of the invasions, see Vol. 2, pp. 143 for Central Pacific Theater.

4. Goodenough, Simon. War Maps: World War II from September 1939 to August 1945, Air, Sea, and Land, Battle by Battle. New York: St. Martin's Press, 1982. 192 pp.
232 maps with supporting text.

5. Mourer, Edgar A., and Martha Rajchmar. Global War: An Atlas of World Strategy. Washington: Infantry Journal Press, 1944. 128 pp.
PCarlMH
Review of the war intended for American service men.

6. Natkiel, Richard. Atlas of American Wars. New York: Arch Cape Books, 1986. 160 pp.   DLC
General campaign maps, including the Marianas, with accompanying narrative.

11

7. Palmer, Robert R., editor. Rand McNally Atlas of World History. New York: Rand McNally Co., ca1965. 216 pp. DLC
Detailed atlas with explanatory comments on each map.

8. Shepherd, William R., editor. Shepherd's Historical Atlas. 9th Edition. New York: Barnes & Noble, 1963.
Provides very brief review of the campaign, particularly useful for pre-war maps.

9. Stembridge, Jasper H. The Oxford War Atlas. New York: Oxford Univ. Press, 1941-1946. 4 vols.
Comprehensive series of maps.

10. U.S. Navy, Hydrographic Office. Gazetteer (No. 6) Caroline, Marianas, Marshall and Gilbert Islands. Second Edition. Washington: Government Printing Office, 1944. 133 pp. DLC
Alphabetical listing of geographic feature names, including islands, villages, cities, rivers, reefs, mountains, bays, atolls, etc. Provides geographic coordinates for locating them.

11. _____ Gazetteer (No. 7) Islands of the Central and South Pacific. Washington: Government Printing Office, 1944. 222 pp. DLC
Alphabetical listing of geographic feature names, including islands, villages, cities, rivers, reefs, mountains, bays, atolls, etc. Provides geographic coordinates for locating them.

12. U.S. War Dept., General Staff. Atlas of the World Battle Fronts in Semi-monthly Phases, to August 1945: Supplement to Biennial Report of Chief of Staff of U.S. Army, July 1, 1943 to June 30, 1945, To Secretary of War. Washington: 1945. 101 pp.
Excellent series of maps clearly showing the Central Pacific operations.

13. A War Atlas for Americans. New York: Simon & Schuster, 1944. 86 pp. PCarlMH
Typical of information available to the general public at the time.

14. Young, Pete, editor. Atlas of the Second World War. New York: G. P. Putnam's Sons, 1974. 288 pp. PCarlMH
Collection of simplified maps with brief text.

BIBLIOGRAPHIES

15. Albion, Robert G. Naval & Maritime History, Annotated Bibliography. 3rd Edition. Mystic, CT: Marine Historical Assoc., 1963. 230 pp. DLC
Comprehensive listing by subject matter, strong emphasis on non-military aspects.

16. _____ First Supplement, 1963-65. Mystic, CT: Marine Historical Assoc., ca1966. 62 pp. DLC

17. _____ Second Supplement, 1965-1968. Mystic, CT: Marine Historical Assoc., ca1969. 60 pp. DLC

GENERAL REFERENCE WORKS   13

18. American Committee on the History of the Second World War. <u>A Select Bibliography of Books on the Second World War: In English published in the United States, 1966-1975</u>. San Francisco: Funk, 1975.
Listing of titles arranged by subject.

19. <u>Air University Library Index to Military Periodicals</u>. Maxwell Air Force Base, AL: Vol. 1, 1949-. DLC
Annual listing by subject.

20. Barnard, Roy, and others. <u>The Era of World War II. General Reference Works, Biography</u>. Washington: Government Printing Office, 1977. 185 pp. (Military History Institute Special Bibliography No. 16, Vol. 2) PCarlMH
Listing of those titles located in the Institute's collection at Carlisle Barracks, Pa.

21. Baylias, Gwyn, editor. <u>Bibliographic Guide to the Two World Wars</u>. New York: Bowker, 1978. 578 pp. DLC
Annotated listing of English language titles.

22. Bloomberg, Marty, and Hans H. Webber. <u>World War II and Its Origins, A Select Bibliography of Books in English</u>. Littleton, CO: Libraries Unlimited, 1975. 311 pp.

23. Cline, Marjorie W., and others, editors. <u>Scholar's Guide to Intelligence Literature: Bibliography of the Russell J. Bowen Collection in the Joseph Mark Lauinger Memorial Library Georgetown University</u>. Frederick, MD: University Publications of America, 1983. 236 pp. DLC
Comprehensive listing by subject.

24. Constantinides, George C. <u>Intelligence and Espionage: An Analytical Bibliography</u>. Boulder, CO: Westview Press, 1983. 559 pp. DLC
Comprehensive listing of titles by subject and indexed.

25. Controvich, James T. <u>United States Army Unit Histories: A Reference and Bibliography</u>. Manhattan, KS: Military Affairs/Aerospace Historian Pubs., 1983. 591 pp. DLC
Comprehensive listing of unit and command histories, plus assortment of reference chapters dealing with order of battles, lineages, organic units of divisions, etc.

26. _____ <u>1987 Supplement</u>. Manhattan, KS: Military Affairs/Aerospace Historian Pubs., 1987. 131 pp. DLC
Provides an additional 1000 titles to the 1983 entry.

27. Cresswell, Mary Ann, and Carl Berger, comp. <u>United States Air Force History: An Annotated Bibliography</u>. Washington: Government Printing Office, 1971. 106 pp. DLC
Annotated bibliography of books and periodical articles arranged by subject.

28. Dornbusch, Charles E. **Unit Histories, Personal Narratives, United States Army. A Checklist.** Cornwallville, NY: Hope Farm Press, 1967. 402 pp. DLC
Listing by unit of army ground units.

29. Funk, Arthur L. **The Second World War: A Select Bibliography of Books in English since 1975.** Claremont, CA: Regina Books, 1985. 210 pp.
Listing of titles by subject.

30. Hilliard, Jack B., and Harold A. Bivins. **An Annotated Reading List of United States Marine Corps History.** Revised edition. Washington: Historical Division, HQ, U.S. Marine Corps, 1971. 55 pp. DN
Annotated listing by subject.

31. International Commission for the Teaching of History. **The Two World Wars. Selective Bibliography.** New York: Pergamon Press, 1965. 246 pp.

32. Kondo, Shinji. **Japanese Military History: A Guide to the Literature.** New York: Garland Pub. Co., 1984. 88 pp.
Annotated bibliography of 437 entries.

33. Miller, Lester L., Jr., and others. **Checklist of Artillery Organizational Histories: A Compilation. Special Bibliography no. 81.** Fort Sill, OK: U.S. Army Field Artillery School Library, 1982. 201 pp. Mimeo.
Provides a comprehensive listing artillery unit histories including many after action reports found in the Artillery School Library.

34. Moran, John B. **Creating a Legend: The Complete Record of Writings about the United States Marine Corps.** Chicago: Moran, Andrews, 1973. 681 pp. DN
Many references to Central Pacific Operations, weak on bibliographic detail.

35. Morton, Louis. **Writings on World War II.** Washington: Service Center for Teachers of History, 1967. 54 pp. DLC
Arranged by subject matter and indexed, intended for high school teacher use.

36. O´Quinlivan, Michael, and Jack B. Hilliard. **An Annotated Bibliography of the United States Marine Corps in the Second World War.** Washington: Historical Division, HQ, U.S.M.C., 1965. 42 pp. DN
Annotated listing of marine-naval titles listed by subject and battles.

37. Pappas, George S. **United States Army Unit Histories.** Carlisle Barracks, PA: U.S. Army Military History Collection, 1971. 404 pp. (Special Bibliographic Series, no. 4) PCarlMH
Listing of the unit history collection at Carlisle Barracks and the Center for Military History in Washington.

GENERAL REFERENCE WORKS 15

38. _____ _____ Carlisle Barracks, PA: U.S. Army Military History Institute, 1978. 2 vols. (Special Bibliographic Series, no. 4, revised and updated) PCarlMH
Listing of the unit history holdings of only the Military History Institute Library.

39. Smith, Myron J., Jr. World War II at Sea: A Bibliography of Sources in English. Vol. 2: The Pacific Theater. Metuchen, NJ: Scarecrow Press, 1976. 427 pp. DLC
Comprehensive annotated listing by subject, indexed by author and subject.

40. _____ Air War Bibliography, 1939-1945: English Language Sources. Vol. 2, The Pacific Theater. Manhattan, KS: Military Affairs/Aerospace Historian Pub., 1978. 329 pp. DLC
Comprehensive listing by subject.

41. Spier, Henry O., comp. World War II in Our Magazines and Books. September 1939 to September 1945, a Bibliography. New York: Stuyvesant Press, 1945. 96 pp.

42. U.S. Army, Office of Military History. Guide to Japanese Monographs and Japanese Studies in Manchuria, 1945-1960. Washington: 1962. 282 pp. CMH
Useful listing and annotation of entire series of reports.

43. _____ United States Army in World War II: Master Index. Readers Guide. Washington: Government Printing Office, 1960. 145 pp.
PCarlMH
Guide and index of volumes in the series published to date including all the Central Pacific volumes.

44. U.S. Naval History Division. United States Naval History: A Bibliography. 6th Edition. Washington: Government Printing Office, 1972. 92 pp. DN
Annotated listing, including a chapter concerning World War II with many entries relating to the Central Pacific.

45. Ziegler, Janet., comp. World War II: Books in English, 1945-65. Stanford, CA: Hoover Institution Press, 1971, 194 pp. DLC
Comprehensive listing of titles arranged by subject matter.

RESEARCH AIDS

46. Allard, Dean C. United States Naval History Sources in the Washington Area and Suggested Research Subjects. 3rd Edition. Washington: Naval History Division [Government Printing Office], 1970. 82 pp. DN
Identifies and describes naval history holdings in the Washington area, including WWII records.

16 THE CENTRAL PACIFIC CAMPAIGN, 1943-1944

47. Cochran, Alexander S., Jr. <u>MAGIC Diplomatic Summaries: A Cochran, Alexander S., Jr. Chronological Finding Aid</u>. New York: Garland, 1981. 139 pp. DLC

48. _____. "Magic," "Ultra," and the Second World War: Literature, Sources, and Outlook." <u>Military Affairs</u>, XLVI (Apr. 1982), pp. 88-92. PCarlMH

49. Frank, Benis M. "Notable Amphibious Doctrine Papers Given to Center." <u>Fortitudine</u>, XVIII (Winter 1988-1989), pp. 16-18. DN
Article concerning the Jeter A. Isely and Philip A. Crowl resource materials donated to the USMC Historical Center.

50. <u>Guide to the National Archives of the United States</u>. Washington: National Archives and Record Service [Government Printing Office], 1974. 884 pp. DLC
Invaluable reference concerning the holdings with descriptions of the various record groups.

51. Handlin, Oscar and others. <u>Harvard Guide to American History</u>. Cambridge, MA: Belknap Press, 1963. 689 pp. DLC
Strong emphasis on the non-military aspects.

52. Higham, Robin, editor. <u>A Guide to the Sources of Military History</u>. Hampden, CT: Archon Books, 1975. 559 pp. DLC
Collection of articles providing a review of recent books worthy of mention.

53. _____. <u>Official Histories. Essays and Bibliographies from around the World</u>. Manhattan, KS: Kansas State Univ. Press, 1970. 644 pp. DLC
Excellent review of the official history programs, includes U.S. and Japan.

54. Higham, Robin, and Donald J. Mrozek, editors. <u>A Guide to the Sources of Military History, Supplement I</u>. Hampden, CT: Archon Books, 1981. 300 pp. DLC
Collection of articles providing a review of recent books worthy of mention.

55. _____. <u>A Guide to the Sources of Military History, Supplement II</u>. Hampden, CT: Archon Books, 1986. 332 pp. DLC
Collection of articles providing a review of recent books worthy of mention.

56. Millett, Allan R. "Research Sources for Marine Corps History." <u>Fortitudine</u>, X (Spring 1981), pp. 10-12. DN
Brief review of public and private holdings concerning Marine Corps history.

57. O'Neill, James E. <u>World War II. An Account of Documents</u>. Washington: Howard Univ. Press, 1976. 269 pp. (National Archives Conferences, Vol. 8) DLC
Collection of essays and commentary concerning the WWII record holdings.

GENERAL REFERENCE WORKS   17

58. Paszek, Lawrence J., comp. United States Air Force History: A Guide to Documentary Sources. Washington: Office of Air Force History, 1973. 254 pp. DLC
Useful source for locating federal and privately held sources concerning the U.S. Army Air Forces.

59. Poulton, Helen J., and Marguerie S. Howland. The Historian's Handbook. A Descriptive Guide to Reference Works. Norman: Univ. of Oklahoma Press, 1972. 304 pp. DLC
Excellent review of primary reference sources and guides.

60. U.S. National Archives and Records Service. Federal Records of World War II. Vol. 2, Military Agencies. Washington: Government Printing Office, 1951. 1061 pp. PCarlMH
Primary reference concerning the National Archives includes analytical descriptions of military record holdings.

61. U.S. Naval History Division, Operational Archives. Partial Checklist World War II Histories and Historical Reports in the Naval History Division: A Partial Checklist. Washington: 1973. 226 pp. ND
Compilation of annotated sources with emphasis on the administrative commands.

62. U.S. Navy Department Library. Guide to United States Naval Administrative Histories of World War II. Washington: 1976. 219 pp. ND
Excellent source providing annotated entries for 173 unpublished reports.

63. Wallace, David, comp. The MAGIC Documents: Summaries and Transcripts of the Top-Secret Diplomatic Communications of Japan, 1938-1945, a Subject and Name Index to. Washington, DC: University Pub. of America, 1980. 14 reels of microfilm. DLC
Comprehensive source material and documents.

NEWSPAPER INDICES

64. Detroit News. War...in Headlines of the Detroit News, 1939-1945. Detroit: 1945. 104 pp. DLC

65. Fortune, Charles H. The War in Retrospect: A Day-to-Day Record of World War II. Dunedin, New Zealand: Evening Star Co., 1944-1945. 2 vols.

66. Merley, David, editor. The Daily Telegraph Story of the War. London: Hodder and Stoughton, 1942-1946. 5 vols.
War coverage of the London Daily Telegraph.

67. New York Herald Tribune. Front Page History of the Second World War, including Historically-Important Photographs of Leading War Personalities and Incidents. A Chronology of Events, and Articles of Surrender. New York: 1946. 112 pp.

68. St. Joseph News-Press. <u>The History of World War II, as told in the Headlines, Maps and Cartoons from St. Joseph News-Press and St. Joseph Gazette, St. Joseph, Missouri</u>. St. Joseph: 1946. 264 pp.

69. San Francisco Examiner. <u>History of the War in Front Pages: Actual Reproductions of Newspaper Front Pages, Selected from the San Francisco Examiner, covering Major Events in World War II, plus complete text of United Nations San Francisco Charter and Statute of World Court</u>. San Francisco: 1945. 61 pp.

70. <u>The Stars and Stripes. World War II Front Pages</u>. New York: Hugh Lauter Leven Assocs., 1985. DLC
Front pages from various notable issues.

3.
General Histories

GENERAL TITLES

71. Agnew, James B. "From Where Did Our Amphibious Doctrine Come?" Marine Corps Gazette, LXIII (Aug. 1979), pp. 52-59. DN
Review of the development of amphibious techniques used in the Pacific Campaigns.

72. Bahrenburg, Bruce. The Pacific: Then and Now. New York: G. P. Putnam's Sons, 1971. 318 pp. PCarlMH
Series of before and after photographs of the various battlefields.

73. Barker, A. J. Japanese Army Handbook, 1939-1945. New York: Hippocrene Books, 1979. 128 pp. DLC
Useful pictorial review of weapons, equipment, and organization.

74. Bergamini, David. Japan's Imperial Conspiracy. New York: William Morrow, 1971. 1239 pp. PCarlMH
Comprehensive review of the Japanese policy formation during the War.

75. Berry, Henry. Semper Fi, Mac: Living Memories of the U.S. Marines in World War II. New York: Arbor House, 1982. 375 pp. DLC
Firsthand accounts.

76. Bishop, John. "Sniper Ship on the Seaway to Tokyo." Saturday Evening Post, CCXVII (Nov. 11, 1944). pp. 20+. DLC
General account of fire support during Saipan and Tinian operations.

77. Blakeney, Ben B. "The Japanese High Command; Part 1, The Organization." Military Affairs, IX (1954), pp. 95-113: "The Japanese High Command Concluded." pp. 208-218. PCarlMH
Comprehensive study of the Japanese command structure and biographies of general officers.

20   THE CENTRAL PACIFIC CAMPAIGN, 1943-1944

78. Blakeney, Jane. <u>Heroes, U.S. Marine Corps, 1861-1955</u>. Washington: Blakeney Pubs., 1957. 621 pp. DLC
Listing of decorations and unit honors awarded to Marine personnel including the WWII period.

79. Brooks, Lester. <u>Behind Japan's Surrender: The Secret That Ended an Empire</u>. New York: McGraw-Hill Book Co., 1968. 428 pp. DLC

80. Brower, Charles F. "Assault or Siege: The Debate over Final Strategy for the Defeat of Japan, 1943-1945. <u>Joint Perspective</u>, II (Spring 1982), pp. 72-83. DLC

81. Burne, Alfred H. <u>Strategy in World War II</u>. Harrisburg: Military Service Pub., 1947. 91 pp. DLC
British views concerning the War's strategy touching on the Central Pacific.

82. Burton, Earl. <u>By Sea and By Land. The Story of Our Amphibious Forces</u>. New York: Whittlesey House, [McGraw-Hill Book Co.], 1944. 218 pp. DLC
Review of the services and equipment used. Wartime censorship limits the usefulness of the information.

83. Byas, Hugh. <u>The Japanese Enemy: His Power and Vulnerability</u>. New York: Alfred A. Knopf, 1942. 107 pp. PCarlMH
General account of military and political situation.

84. Bykofsky, Joseph, and Harold Larson. <u>The Transportation Corps: Operation Overseas</u>. Washington: Office of the Chief of Military History [Government Printing Office], 1957. 671 pp. (United States Army in World War II, Technical Services) PCarlMH
Comprehensive review of activities in the Pacific and European Theaters of Operation.

85. Cant, Gilbert. <u>The Great Pacific Victory from the Solomons to Tokyo</u>. New York: John Day Co., 1945. 407 pp. PCarlMH
General history surpassed by more recent titles.

86. Cave, Hugh B. <u>We Build, We Fight! The Story of the Seabees</u>. New York: Harper & Bros., 1944. 122 pp. DLC
General history lacking detail due to wartime censorship.

87. Champie, Elmore A. <u>A Brief History of the Marine Corps Recruit Depot, Paris Island, South Carolina, 1891-1962</u>. Washington: Historical Branch, HQ, U.S.M.C., 1962. (Marine Corps Historical Reference Series, No. 8) DN
Contains a review of the WWII training activities at Paris Island, pp. 9-12.

88. Clausen, Walter B. <u>Blood for the Emperor. A Narrative History of the Human Side of the War in the Pacific</u>. New York: Appleton-Century Co., 1943. 341 pp. DLC
Collection of stories lacking detail due to wartime censorship, including a description of Carlson's Raiders and the 1942 Makin raid.

GENERAL HISTORIES 21

89. Coffey, Thomas M. *Imperial Tragedy. Japan in World War II, the First Days and the Last.* New York: World Pub. Co., 1970. 531 pp. DLC
Comments on impact of bombing raids from Marianas.

90. CBS [Columbia Broadcasting System] War Correspondents. *From Pearl Harbor into Tokyo.* New York: Columbia Broadcasting Systems, 1945. 312 pp. PCarlMH
Collection of reports prepared by CBS Correspondents concerning the War in the Pacific.

91. Collier, Basil. *Japan at War: An Illustrated History of the War in the Far East, 1931-1945.* London: Sidgwick & Jackson, 1975. 192 pp. DLC
Pictorial history from British perspective including Central Pacific.

92. _____ *The War in the Far East, 1941-1945.* New York: William Morrow & Co., 1969. 518 pp. PCarlMH
Excellent summary of the War in the Pacific with emphasis on the Southeast Asia Theater and the British participation.

93. Condit, Kenneth W., and John H. Johnstone. *A Brief History of Marine Corps Staff Organization.* Washington: Historical Div., HQ, U.S.M.C., 1963. (Marine Corps Historical Reference Series, no. 25) DN
Useful review of the U.S.M.C. Headquarters.

94. Condit, Kenneth W., and others. *Marine Corps Ground Training in World War II.* Washington: Historical Branch, Headquarters, U.S.M.C., 1956. 353 pp. DN
Comprehensive description of the training of Marine personnel during the war.

95. Conner, Howard. "Cannoneers Post!" *Leatherneck*, XXVII (Dec. 1944), pp. 40-44. DN
Brief history of Marine Corps artillery in the Pacific.

96. Cook, Charles D., Jr. "The Pacific Command Divided: The ´Most Unexplainable´ Decision." *United States Naval Institute Proceedings*, CIV (Sept. 1978), pp. 55-61. DN
Review of the dual command structure in the Pacific theater.

97. Costello, John. *The Pacific War.* New York: Rawson, Wade Pubs., 1981. 742 pp. DLC
Journalistic account of the war.

98. Crane, Aimee. *Marines at War.* New York: Hyperion Press, 1943. 128 pp. DLC
Review of the Marine combat artists in the Pacific along with biographical sketches of the artist and reproductions of art works.

99. Creswell, John. <u>Generals and Admirals: The Story of Amphibious Command</u>. London: Longman, Green, 1952. DN
Review of the relationships between Marine and Naval commanders in the Pacific, pp. 172-188.

100. Dixon, Joe C., editor. <u>The American Military and the Far East. Proceedings of the Ninth Military History Symposium, United States Air Force Academy, 1 - 3 October 1980</u>. Washington: Government Printing Office, 1980. 318 pp. DLC
Collection of essays concerning the Far East with many references to the Central Pacific.

101. Dod, Karl C. <u>The Corps of Engineers: The War against Japan</u>. Washington: Office of the Chief of Military History [Government Printing Office], 1966. 759 pp. (U.S. Army in World War II, Technical Services) PCarlMH
Comprehensive review of engineer operations in the Pacific.

102. Dower, John W. <u>War Without Mercy. Race & Power in the Pacific War</u>. New York: Pantheon Books, 1986. 399 pp. DLC
Impact of race on American and Japanese operations in WWII.

103. Earle, Edward M., editor. <u>Makers of Modern Strategy</u>. Princeton, NJ: Princeton Univ. Press, 1943. 553 pp. DLC
Compilation of essays including Alexander Kiralfy's "Japanese Naval Strategy", pp. 457-484.

104. Ehrman, John. <u>Grand Strategy, Volume 5, August 1943-September 1944</u>. J. R. M. Butler, editor. London: Her Majesty's Stationery Office, 1956. 634 pp. (United Kingdom Military Series, History of the Second World War) PCarlMH
Includes a review of the Central Pacific campaign as seen from the British perspective.

105. Erskine, John C. "Language Officers Recall Combat Roles in the Pacific." <u>Fortitudine</u>, XII (Spring 1986), pp. 23-24. DN
Account of officers who tried to coach Japanese into surrendering.

106. Fabyamic, Thomas A. "A Critique of United States Air War Planning, 1941-1944." unpublished PhD Dissertation, St. Louis Univ., 1973. 218 lvs. MoSU
Account of air war planning concentrating on the European phases.

107. <u>Factual Chart of World War II Asiatic-Pacific Operations</u>. Lebanon, PA: World War Chart Co., n.d. (Broadside 57 x 38 inches)
Provides color insignia and brief reviews of each campaign in the Central Pacific.

108. Falk, Stanley L. "Japanese Strategy in World War II." <u>Military Review</u>, XLII (June 1962), pp. 70-81. PCarlMH
Excellent account of Japanese strategy during the war.

GENERAL HISTORIES 23

109. Feis, Herbert. <u>Churchill, Roosevelt, Stalin: The War They Waged and the Peace They Sought</u>. Princeton, NJ: Princeton Univ. Press, 1957. DLC
Excellent review of the interactions between the Allied political leadership.

110. Fleisher, Wilfred. <u>Our Enemy Japan</u>. Garden City, NY: Doubleday, Doran & Co., 1943. 236 pp. DLC
Review of the prewar military and economic situation for the general reader.

111. Florance, Charles W., Jr. <u>Organization of the Southwest Pacific Area and Pacific Ocean Areas</u>. Washington: 1946. 7 pp. PCarlMH
Lecture presented at Army and Navy Staff College.

112. Fuller, John F. C. <u>The Second World War, 1939-1945. A Strategic and Tactical History</u>. New York: Duell Sloan, and Pearce, 1954. 431 pp. DLC

113. Giffin, William, editor. <u>Command and Commanders in Modern Military History. The Proceeding of the Second Military History Symposium, U.S. Air Force Academy, 2-3 May 1968</u>. Washington: Government Printing Office, 1969. DLC
Naval leaders in World War II, pp. 207-250; a discussion of the command styles of the naval leaders including Adm. Raymond Spruance.

114. Gordon, Gary. <u>The Rise and Fall of the Japanese Empire</u>. Derby, CT: Monarch Books, 1962. 236 pp.

115. Graybar, Lloyd J. "The Japanese Way of War, 1941-1945." <u>Air University Review</u>, XX (May-June 1985), pp. 105-108. AMAU
Compilation of book reviews concerning Japanese at war.

116. Great Britain. Admiralty Personal Services Department. <u>The Enemy Japan</u>. Great Britain: Admiralty Personal Services Department, 1944. 125 pp. PCarlMH
Twelve essays for British Forces concerning the Japanese.

117. Greenfield, Kent R. <u>American Strategy in World War II, a Reconsideration</u>. Baltimore: Johns Hopkins Univ. Press, 1963. 145 pp. PCarlMH
Emphasizes the Army's contribution to the war strategy.

118. _____ <u>The Historian and the Army</u>. New Brunswick, NJ: Rutgers Univ. Press, 1954. 93 pp. PCarlMH
Interesting review of the Army's history program that led to the preparation of the official history of the war including the Pacific operations.

119. _____, editor. <u>Command Decisions</u>. New York: Harcourt Brace and Co., 1959. 481 pp. PCarlMH
Collection of essays regarding strategic decisions of WWII, "Luzon versus Formosa", pp. 358-373, by Robert R. Smith contains a review of the strategic issues facing the Pacific leaders in 1944.

120. Guillain, Robert. I Saw Tokyo Burning. An Eyewitness Narrative from Pearl Harbor to Hiroshima. Translated by William Byron. Garden City: Doubleday, 1981. 298 pp. DLC
Written by a French reporter in Japan during the War.

121. Hanrahan, Gene Z., editor. Assault! True Action Stories of the Island War in the Pacific. New York: Berkeley, 1962. 255 pp. DLC
Firsthand account of various invasions including the Central Pacific operations.

122. Hara, Tomio, and Akira Takeuchi. Japanese Tanks and Fighting Vehicles. Tokyo: Shuppan Kyodo, 1961. 2 vols.
Comprehensive photographic account, text in Japanese, photo captions in English.

123. Harrison, John A. "The USSR, Japan and the End of the Great Pacific War." Parameters, XIV (Feb. 1984), pp. 76-87. DN
Diplomatic history based on Japanese wartime communications.

124. Hashimoto, Mochitura. Sunk! The Story of the Japanese Submarine Fleet, 1941-1945. Translated by E. H. M. Colegrave. New York: Henry Holt, 1954. 276 pp. DLC
Review of Japanese submarine operations by one of its submarine commanders.

125. Havens, Thomas R. H. Valley of Darkness: The Japanese People and World War II. New York: W. W. Norton & Co., 1978. 280 pp. DLC
Detailed account of Japanese home front during the war.

126. Hayashi, Saburo, in collaboration with Alvin D. Coox. Kogun. The Japanese Army in the Pacific War. Quantico, VA: Marine Corps Assoc., 1959. 249 pp. DLC
One of the best studies from the Japanese perspective, includes a biographical listing of Japanese Army general officers.

127. Hayes, Grace P. The History of the Joint Chiefs of Staff in World War II. The War Against Japan. Annapolis, MD: Naval Institute Press, 1982. 964 pp. DN
Considered the best account of the wartime activities of JCS concerning the War in the Pacific.

128. Heavy, William F. Down Ramp: The Story of the Army Amphibian Engineers. Washington: Infantry Journal Press, 1947. 272 p. PCarlMH
Excellent source concerning amphibian engineer operations.

129. Heigo. Organization of the Japanese Army. n.p.: 1942. 128 pp. PCarlMH

130. Heinl, Robert D., Jr. Soldiers of the Sea: A Definitive History of the United States Marine Corps, 1775-1962. Annapolis, MD: Naval Institute Press, 1962. 693 pp. DN
Readable history of the Marine Corps including the Central Pacific Campaigns.

GENERAL HISTORIES 25

131. Hit the Beach: Your Marine Corps in Action... New York: Wise, 1948. 386 pp.
Pictorial history of the Marines operations in World War II.

132. Holmes, Wilfred J. Double Edged Secrets, U.S. Naval Intelligence in the Pacific during World War II. Annapolis: Naval Institute Press, 1979. 232 pp. DN
Excellent account of intelligence operations in the Central Pacific Campaigns including accounts of the information obtained in the Central Pacific.

133. Hough, Frank O. The Island War. The United States Marines in the Pacific War. New York: Lippincott Co., 1947. 413 pp. DLC
Excellent review and analysis of the amphibious operations in the Pacific.

134. Hoyt, Edwin P. Japan's War, the Great Pacific Conflict, 1853 to 1952. New York: McGraw-Hill Book Co., 1986. 514 pp. DLC
Comprehensive account drawing heavily on Japanese sources.

135. Huie, William B. Can Do! The Story of the Seabees. New York: E. P. Dutton and Co., 1944. 250 pp. DN
Review of the naval construction unit operations, suffers from wartime censorship.

136. _____ From Omaha to Okinawa, the Story of the Seabees. New York: E. P. Dutton and Co., 1945. 257 pp. DN
Review of the activities and services of the naval construction units.

137. _____ Seabees Roads to Victory, a Brochure of Maps Depicting the World-wide Activities of the Naval Construction Battalions. New York: E. P. Dutton and Co., 1944. 16 lvs.
Series of maps of limited usefulness due to wartime censorship.

138. Hurley, Alfred F., and Robert C. Ehrhart, editors. Air Power and War. Proceedings of the Eighth Military History Symposium, United States Air Force Academy, 18-20 May 1978. Washington: Government Printing Office, 1979. 461 pp. DLC
Collection of essays and commentary including Coox's "Rise and Fall of the Imperial Japanese Air Forces," pp. 84-95.

139. Ienaga, Saburo. The Pacific War, World War II and the Japanese, 1931-1945. New York: Pantheon Books, 1978. 316 pp. DLC
Review of how and why the Japanese fought the war.

140. Ingraham, Reg. First Fleet, the Story of the U.S. Coast Guard at War. Indianapolis: Bobbs-Merrill Co., 1944. 309 pp. DLC
Wartime account of limited usefulness due to censorship.

141. Iriye, Akua. Power and Culture: The Japanese-American War, 1941-1945. Cambridge: Harvard Univ. Press, 1981. 304 pp. DLC
Review of the war as clash of cultures and social systems providing new material on Japan's wartime relationships with the Soviet Union and China.

26 THE CENTRAL PACIFIC CAMPAIGN, 1943-1944

142. Isely, Jeder A., and Philip A. Crowl. The U.S. Marines and Amphibious War. Its Theory, Its Practice in the Pacific War. Princeton, NJ: Princeton Univ. Press, 1951. 636 pp. DN
Excellent account of the development of amphibious assault operations tactics, reviewing each of the major assaults and the lessons learned and applied.

143. James, D. Clayton, and Anne S. Wells. A Time for Giants. Politics of the American High Command in World War II. New York: Franklin Watts, 1987. 317 pp. DLC
Review of the American high command including Nimitz, MacArthur, and Spruance, providing insight to their interpersonal relationships.

144. James, David H. The Rise and Fall of the Japanese Empire. New York: Macmillan, 1951. 409 pp. DLC
General account of the Pacific war.

145. The Jap Soldier. Washington: Infantry Journal Press, 1943. 124 pp. PCarlMH
Issued to the troops to familiarize them with the Japanese forces.

146. Karig, Walter, and others. Battle Report: The End of an Empire. New York: Farrar & Reinhart, 1948. 532 pp. DN
General history with heavy emphasis on naval and marine operations in the Pacific, including the Gilberts, Marshalls, and Marianas Operations.

147. Kase, Toshikazu. Journey to the Missouri. Edited by Dave N. Rose. New Haven: Yale Univ. Press, 1950. 282 pp. DN
Author was Foreign Office official in Tokyo.

148. Kato, Masuo. The Lost War: A Japanese Reporter's Inside Story. New York: Alfred A. Knopf, 1946. 264 pp. PCarlMH
War as seen through a Japanese reporter's eyes.

149. Keesing, Marie M. Pacific Islands in War and Peace. New York: Institute of Pacific Relations, 1944. 64 pp. PCarlMH

150. Leckie, Robert. Strong Men Armed: The United States Marines Against Japan. New York: Random House, 1962. 563 pp. DN
Popular history with emphasis on individual accounts.

151. Lieghton, Richard, and Robert W. Croatley. Global Logistics and Strategy, 1940-1943. Washington: Office of the Chief of Military History [Government Printing Office], 1955. 780 pp. (United States Army in World War II, War Department) DN
Comprehensive review of the strategic and tactical considerations related to logistical issues.

152. Lewin, Ronald. The American Magic: Codes, Ciphers and the Defeat of Japan. New York: Farrar, Straus, Giroux, 1982. 332 pp. DN
Review of American code breaking efforts during the Pacific War based on newly declassified materials and documents.

GENERAL HISTORIES 27

153. Lewis, Charles L. Famous American Marines. Boston: Page, 1950. 375 pp. DN
Series of biographies including Generals Holland Smith and Roy S. Geiger.

154. Lindsay, Robert G. This High Name: Public Relations and the U.S. Marine Corps. Madison, WI: Univ. of Wisconsin Press, 1956. 101 pp. DN
History of the Marine Corps public relations program including its Second World War activities.

155. Lory, Hillis. Japan's Wartime Masters: The Army in Japanese Life. New York: Viking Press, 1943. 256 pp. PCarlMH
Review of Japanese military philosophy based on pre-war observations.

156. Lucus, James. Combat Correspondent. New York: Reynal and Hitchcock, 1944. 210 pp.
Experiences of a war correspondent with the Marines in Boot Camp and service on Tarawa.

157. Macintyre, Donald G. F. W. The Battle for the Pacific. London: Batsford, 1966. 240 pp.
Popular history for general reader.

158. Madej, W. Victor. Japanese Armed Forces Order of Battle. Allentown, PA: Game Pub. Co., 1981. 2 vols. DLC
Compilation of tables and maps.

159. _____ Japanese War Mobilization and the Pacific Campaigns, 1939-1945. Allentown, PA: Game Pub. Co., 1985. 192 pp. DLC
Compilation of maps and statistical tables concerning Japanese war effort.

160. _____ U.S Army Order of Battle, 1941-1945: Pacific Theater. Allentown, PA: Game Pub. Co., 1984. DLC
Compilation of tables and maps.

161. _____ U.S. Army and Marine Corps Order of Battle, Pacific Theater Supplement. Allentown, PA: Game Pub. Co., 1984. DLC
Compilation of tables and maps.

162. Markham, George. Japanese Infantry Weapons in World War Two. New York: Hippocrene Books, 1976. 96 pp. DLC
Brief pictorial review of Japanese infantry weapons.

163. Martin, Ralph G. World War II: A Photographic Record of the War in the Pacific from Pearl Harbor to V-J Day. Greenwich, CT: Fawcett Publications, 1965. 224 pp. DLC

164. Masher, John S. Intelligence in Amphibious Operations. Washington: 1945. 24 pp. PCarlMH
Central Pacific campaigns are used as examples.

165. Matherson, Daniel M., editor. Naval History, The Sixth Symposium of the U.S. Naval Academy. Wilmington, DE: Scholarly Resources, 1987. 376 pp. DLC
Includes article by Mary Ellen Condon, "Medical Aspects of Amphibious Operations during the War against Japan", pp. 276-288.

166. Matloff, Maurice. Strategic Planning for Coalition Warfare, 1943-1944. Washington: Office of the Chief of Military History [Government Printing Office], 1959. 640 pp. (United States Army in World War II, War Department) DLC
Review including many references to the Central Pacific operations.

167. Maurer, Maurer. "A Delicate Mission: Aerial Reconnaissance of Japanese Islands before World War II." Military Affairs, XXVI (Summer 1962), pp. 66-75. DLC
Account of one of the early reconnaissance missions over Japanese-held islands.

168. Maxon, Yale C. Control of Japanese Foreign Policy: A Study in Civil-Military Rivalry, 1930-1945. Berkeley: Univ. of California Press, 1957. 286 pp. DLC

169. Mayer, S. L., editor. The Japanese War Machine. Secaucus, NJ: Chartwell Books, 1976. 255 pp.
Pictorial history of the Japanese armed forces during the war with emphasis on the various weapons used.

170. Mercey, Arch A. Sea, Surf and Hell, the U.S. Coast Guard in World War II. New York: Prentice-Hall, 1945. 352 pp. DLC
Collection of previously published articles including many firsthand accounts.

171. Meskill, Johanna M. Hitler and Japan: The Hollow Alliance. New York: Atherton Press, 1966. 245 pp. DLC
Review of economic and military cooperation.

172. Metcalf, Clyde H. The Marine Corps Reader. New York: G. P. Putnam, 1944. 600 pp. DLC
Collection of essays concerning individual Marine recollections.

173. Montross, Lynn. The United States Marines: A Pictorial History. New York: Reinhart, 1959. 242 pp. DN
General pictorial history of the Marines including the World War II period.

174. Morgan, Henry G., Jr. Planning the Defeat of Japan: A Study of Total War Strategy. Washington: Office of the Chief of Military History, 1961. 194 pp. PCarlMH
Comprehensive study Pacific War strategy.

175. Morrison, Samuel E. "Pacific Strategy." Marine Corps Gazette, XLVI (Aug. 1962), pp. 34-40. DN
Brief review.

GENERAL HISTORIES 29

176. _____ Strategy and Compromise. Boston: Little, Brown and Co., 1958. 120 pp. DN
Excellent summary of the strategy adopted by the United States in the Pacific.

177. Morrison, Wilbur H. Above and Beyond, 1941-1945. New York: St. Martin's Press, 1983. 314 pp. DLC
Account based on the reflections of admirals and airmen who participated in the Pacific War.

178. Morton, Louis. "Command in the Pacific, 1941-45." Military Review, XLI (Dec. 1961), pp. 76-88. PCarlMH
Review of the dual command structure.

179. _____ "Japanese Policy and Strategy in Mid-War." United States Naval Institute Proceedings, LXXXV (Feb. 1959), pp. 52+. DN
Review of the Japanese military-political situation during 1943.

180. _____ "The Origins of the Pacific Strategy." Marine Corps Gazette, XLI (Aug. 1957), pp. 36-43. DN
Review of American interests in the Pacific after the Spanish-American War.

181. _____ Pacific Command: A Study of Interservice Relations. Harmon Memorial Lectures in Military History No. 3. Denver, CO: U.S. Air Force Academy, 1961. 29 pp. DLC
Detailed review of divided command in the Pacific Theater.

182. _____ Strategy and Command: The First Two Years. Washington: Office of Chief of Military History [Government Printing Office], 1962. 761 pp. (U.S. Army in World War II, Pacific Theater) PCarlMH
Considered the best account of first two years of the Army's participation in development of strategic plans for the Pacific Theater Operations.

183. Myers, Martin L. Yardbird Myers, the Fouled-Up Leatherneck. Philadelphia: Dorrance, 1944. 230 pp. DLC
Dictionary of contemporary slang used by Marines.

184. Nalty, Bernard C. Marine Corps Officer Procurement: A Brief History. Washington: Historical Branch, Headquarters, U.S.M.C., 1958. 18 pp. DN
Review of officer recruitment and procurement procedures in World War II.

185. _____, and others. United States Marine Corps Ranks and Grades, 1775-1962. Washington: Historical Branch, Headquarters, U.S.M.C., 1962. 45 pp. DN
Brief review of the ranks and grades of the Marines and the effects of World War II on them.

186. Navy Times, editors of. Operation Victory: Winning the Pacific War. New York: G. P. Putnam, 1968. 192 pp. DLC
General history of the War in the Pacific with emphasis on the naval aspects.

187. New York, Museum of Modern Art. Power in the Pacific. New York: U.S. Camera, 1945. 144 pp. DLC
Collection of photographs concerning the Pacific War.

188. O'Sheel, Patrick, and Gene Cook, editors. Semper Fidelis: The U.S. Marines in the Pacific, 1942-1945. New York: William Sloan Assocs., 1947. 360 pp. DLC
General history.

189. Oldfield, Barney. Never a Shot in Anger. New York: Duell, Sloan and Pearce, 1956. 334 pp. DLC
Account of the roles and experiences of war correspondents, includes a roster of all U.S. accredited War Correspondents for the WWII era.

190. "Our Own Baedeker." New Yorker, XX (July 15, 1944), pp. 14-15. DLC
Brief historical background of Marianas Islands.

191. Parker, William D. A Concise History of the United States Marine Corps, 1775-1969. Washington: Government Printing Office, 1971. 143 pp. DN
General history including the Central Pacific Campaigns.

192. Pierce, Philip N., and Frank O. Hough. The Compact History of the United States Marine Corps. New York: Hawthorn Books, 1960. 326 pp. DN
Popular history including coverage of the Central Pacific battles.

193. Pratt, Fletcher. The Marine's War: An Account of the Struggle for the Pacific from both American and Japanese Sources. New York: Sloane, 1948. 456 pp. DN
General account of the Marines participation in the Second World War with much concerning the Central Pacific Drive.

194. Price, Willard. Japan's Islands of Mystery. New York: John Day Co., 1944. 264 pp. DLC
Pre-war tour of Japanese Mandate islands including those in the Marianas.

195. Puleston, W. D. The Armed Forces of the Pacific. A Comparison of the Military and Naval Power of the United States and Japan. New Haven: Yale Univ. Press, 1941. 273 pp. DN
Useful for its pre-war assessments of the forces involved.

196. Reed, George A. "GI's and Samurai: Perspectives of World War II in the Pacific." Air University Review, XX (May-June 1985), pp. 109-113. AMAU
Compilation of annotated book reviews concerning American and Japanese soldiers during the war.

GENERAL HISTORIES 31

197. Robson, Robert W. The Pacific Islands Year Book. Sydney, Australia: Publications, Ltd., 1943. DLC
Descriptive review of the various islands including their histories and geography.

198. _____ The Pacific Islands Year Book, 1944. New York: Macmillan Co., 1945. 371 pp. DLC
Update of the previous title.

199. Rosignoli, Guido. Army Badges and Insignia of World War II. U.S., Great Britain, Poland, Belgium, Italy, U.S.S.R, Germany. New York: Macmillan Co., 1972. 228 pp. DLC
Color plates of unit and rank insignia and anecdotal comments arranged by country.

200. _____ Army Badges and Insignia of World War II. British Commonwealth, Canada, South Africa, British African Territories, India, British Overseas Territories, Finland, France, Japan, Netherlands, Yugoslavia, China, Denmark, Czechoslovakia. New York: Macmillan Co., 1975. 198 pp. DLC
Color plates of unit and rank insignia and anecdotal comments arranged by country.

201. _____ Badges and Insignia of World War II. Air Force, Naval, Marine. New York: Exeter Books, 1983. 363 pp. DLC
Color plates of unit and rank insignia and anecdotal comments arranged by country.

202. _____ Parachute Badges and Insignia of World War II in Colour. London: Blandford Books, 1979. 227 pp. DLC
Color plates of unit and rank insignia and anecdotal comments arranged by country, includes a very brief description of Japanese airborne unit that fought on Saipan as ground troops.

203. Schoun, Karl. U.S. Marine Corps Biographical Dictionary: Fighting Men, What They Did, Where They Served. New York: Watts, 1963. 278 pp. DN
Biographical sketches of famous Marines, including many from the WWII period.

204. _____, editor. The Leathernecks: An Informal History of the U.S. Marine Corps. New York: Watts, 1963. 224 pp. DN
Compilation of articles from Leatherneck, including stories concerning the Marianas operations.

205. Shane, Ted. Heroes of the Pacific. New York: Messner, 1944. 373 pp. DLC
Series of human interest stories concerning the Marines.

206. Sill, Van Rensselaer. American Miracle. The Story of War Construction Around the World. New York: Odyssey Press, 1947. 301 pp. DLC
General review of construction activities of U.S. Forces, including an account of the development of Tinian.

207. Simmons, Edwin. "Marine Corps Logistics in World War II." *Fortitudine*, XVI (Spring 1987), pp. 3-4. DN
Review of the evolving supply efforts during the various invasions.

208. Smith, Gladdis. <u>American Diplomacy during the Second World War, 1941-1945</u>. New York: Wiley, 1965. 194 pp. DLC

209. Snell, John L. <u>Illusion and Necessity: The Diplomacy of Global War, 1939-1945</u>. Boston: Houghton-Mifflin, 1963. 229 pp. DLC

210. Spector, Ronald H. <u>The American War Against Japan. Eagle Against the Sun</u>. New York: Macmillan, 1985. 589 pp. (Macmillan Wars of the United States series) PCarlMH
Concise and readable review of the War in the Pacific.

211. _____, editor. <u>Listening to the Enemy. Key Documents on the Role of Communications Intelligence in the War Against Japan</u>. Wilmington, DE: Scholarly Resources, 1988. 368 pp. DLC
Collection of 21 documents relating to operations against Japan during the war.

212. Stanley, Roy M., II. <u>World War II Photo Intelligence</u>. New York: Charles Scribner's Sons, 1981. 374 pp. DLC
Excellent review of methodologies and equipment used.

213. Stanton, Shelby L. <u>World War II Order of Battle</u>. Novato, CA: Presidio Press, 1984. 620 pp. PCarlMH
Provides useful army unit related information.

214. Stauffer, Alvin P. <u>The Quartermaster Corps: Operations in the War against Japan</u>. Washington: Office of the Chief of Military History [Government Printing Office], 1956. 358 pp. (U.S. Army in World War II, Technical Services) DN
Comprehensive account of the Army Quartermaster Corps in the War against Japan including the Central Pacific operations.

215. Steinberg, Raphael. <u>Island Hopping</u>. Alexandria, VA: Time-Life Books, 1978. 208 pp. DLC
Photographic history of operations in the Pacific.

216. Talbot-Booth, E. C. <u>All the World's Fighting Fleets</u>. New York: D. Appleton-Century Co., 1937. 604 pp. DLC
Useful compilation of ship information with strong emphasis on the British Navy.

217. Tantum, William H., and E. J. Hoffschmidt, editors. <u>Japanese Combat Weapons</u>. Old Greenwich, CT: WE, 1968. 228 pp. DLC
Pictorial review of various Japanese weapons used during the war.

218. TeJen, Yu. <u>The Japanese Struggle for World Empire</u>. New York: Vantage Press, 1967. 330 pp. DLC
Account of the Japanese side of the war.

GENERAL HISTORIES   33

219. Thompson, George R., and Dixie R. Harris. The Signal Corps: The Outcome (Mid-1943 through 1945). Washington: Office of the Chief of Military History [Government Printing Office], 1966. 720 pp. (U.S. Army in World War II, Technical Services) PCarlMH
Comprehensive review, including its operations in the Pacific.

220. Thompson, Paul W., and others. How the Japanese Army Fights. New York: Penguin Publications [Infantry Journal], 1942. 167 pp. DLC
Book given to troops to familiarize them with Japanese tactics and weapons.

221. Tolland, John. The Rising Sun: The Decline and Fall of the Japanese Empire, 1936-1945. New York: Random House, 1970. 707 pp. DLC
Readable and comprehensive history of Pacific War.

222. U.S. Army. Far East Command. War Politics in Japan. n.p.: Far East Command, 1946. 168 pp. PCarlMH
Prepared by the Civil Intelligence Division.

223. U.S. Army Forces in the Central Pacific Area. G-4. World War II Allied and Enemy Action. n.p.: HQ, US Army Forces in the Central Pacific Area, 1943. 10 pp. PCarlMH
Chronology, December 7, 1941 to December 20, 1943.

224. U.S. Army Forces in the Pacific Ocean Areas. 1944 Progress of the War in the Pacific Ocean Areas. n.p.: G-2 AF Mid Pac, ca1944. 70 pp. PCarlMH

225. U.S. Army, Pacific. General Headquarters. Report of Board of Officers convened to study the Japanese Antiaircraft and Seacoast Artillery. n.p.: 1946. 319 pp. PCarlMH
Covers weapons and emplacements.

226. _____ Survey of Japanese Seacoast Artillery. n.p.: 1946. 160 pp. PCarlMH

227. U.S. Department of Army. Office of the Chief of Military History. Order of Battle of the United States Army Ground Forces in World War, Pacific Theater of Operations. Washington: Department of Army, 1959. 697 pp. PCarlMH
Invaluable compilation of regimental and larger units that served in the Pacific Theater providing commanding officers, chronologies, stations, etc.

228. U.S. Army, Military Academy. The War with Japan. West Point, NY: 1944-1946. 3 pts. PCarlMH
Excellent summary with maps of the various campaigns in the Pacific.

229. U.S. Marine Corps, Historical Branch. A Brief History of the Marine Corps Base and Recruit Depot, San Diego, California. Washington: Historical Division, HQ, U.S.M.C., 1960. (Marine Corps Historical Reference Series, no. 20.) DN
Brief review of the activities during the War is included.

34 THE CENTRAL PACIFIC CAMPAIGN, 1943-1944

230. _____ A Chronology of the United States Marine Corps. Washington: Historical Branch, U.S.M.C., 1965-1970. 4 vols. DN
Daily chronology, last two volumes cover the Central Pacific drive.

231. _____ A History of Marine Corps Roles and Missions, 1775-1962. Washington: Historical Branch, U.S.M.C., 1962. 36 pp. (Marine Corps Historical Reference Series, No. 30) DN
Brief review of the laws governing the Marine Corps.

232. U.S. Marine Institute. Marines in Action: A Review of the U.S. Marine Corps' Operations in the Pacific Phase of World War II., from Samoa to Peleliu. Washington: 1945. 61 pp. DN

233. "The United States Marine Corps in World War II." United States Naval Institute Proceedings, LXXIV (Aug. 1948), pp. 1013-1019. DN
Pictorial review.

234. U.S. Navy. Navy Department Communiques 1-300; and Pertinent Press Releases, December 10, 1941-March 5, 1943. Washington: Government Printing Office, 1943. 194 pp. DN
Official releases of Navy-Marine operations for the period mentioned.

235. _____ Navy Department Communiques 1-300; and Pertinent Press Releases, March 6, 1943 to May 24, 1945. Washington: Government Printing Office, 1945. 480 pp. DN
Collection of the official releases of Navy-Marine operations during the War for the period mentioned.

236. U.S. Navy, Bureau of Medicine and Surgery. "The United States Navy Medical Department at War, 1941-1945." unpublished paper: 1945. 2 vols. DN
Comprehensive review of the role of naval medicine in the war.

237. U.S. Navy, Bureau of Yards and Docks. Building the Navy's Bases in World War II: History of the Bureau of Yards and Docks and the Civil Engineer Corps, 1940-1946. Washington: Government Print. Office, 1947. 2 vols. DN
Comprehensive review of the bureau activities in the War.

238. U.S. Navy, Central Pacific, Forward Area. "History of the Supply Department." unpublished paper: Admin. Hist. Appen. 20 (12), n.d. 15 pp. DN
Brief chronology and outline.

239. _____ "Postal Department." unpublished paper: Admin. Hist. Appen. 20 (5), n.d. 7 pp. DN
Brief description of the postal organization and operations in the Pacific.

240. _____ "Staff-General." unpublished paper: Admin. Hist. Appen. 20 (13), n.d. 16 pp. DN
Brief description of the communications, legal, welfare and recreation, chaplain, and educational service departments.

GENERAL HISTORIES   35

241. _____ "Sub-Area Commands." unpublished paper: Admin. Hist. Appen. 20 (14), n.d. 5 pp. DN
Review of the histories of the island and atoll commands during the war.

242. U.S. Navy, Pacific Fleet and Pacific Ocean Area. Change in the Japanese High Command. n.p.: 1944. (CincPac-CincPoa Bulletin 57-44) DN

243. _____ Japanese Army and Navy Land Forces. n.p.: 1943. (Know your Enemy Series, Supplement to the CincPac-CincPoa Weekly Intelligence, Vol. 1, no. 13) DN

244. _____ Japanese Naval Ground Forces. n.p.: 1945. (CincPac-CincPoa Bulletin 11-45) DN

245. _____ Native Labor in Central Pacific Islands to be Occupied. n.p.: 1944. 4 pp. PCarlMH

246. _____ Tables of Organization and Tables of Equipment--Jap Forces. n.p.: 1944. (Know Your Enemy Series, Supplement to Weekly Intelligence, Vol. 1, no. 26) DN

247. U.S. Strategic Bombing Survey. Campaigns of the Pacific War. Washington: Government Printing Office, 1946. 395 pp. DLC
Narrative and map history of the various campaigns.

248. _____ Interrogations of Japanese Officials. Washington: Government Printing Office, 1947. 2 vols. DLC
Collection of postwar interviews of civilian, military and naval leaders concerning military and naval operations.

249. _____ Summary Report (Pacific War). Washington: Government Printing Office, 1946. 32 pp. DLC
Brief history of the Pacific War Campaigns.

250. U.S. War Department. Handbook on Japanese Military Forces. (TM-E-20-480/) Washington: Government Printing Office, 1944. 399 pp. PCarlMH
Excellent study of organization, weapons, and equipment used by the Japanese Army, heavily illustrated.

251. _____ Standard Military Motor Vehicles. Technical Manual No. 9-2800. Washington: War Department, 1943. 560 pp. DLC
Photographs and specifications of each motor vehicle used by the U.S. Army during 1943, arranged by vehicle type.

252. U.S. War Department, Adjutant General's Office. Official Army Register. Jan. 1 1943. Washington: Government Printing Office, 1943. (Issued annually) PCarlMH
Alphabetical listing of Army and Army Air Force officers providing date of birth, rank, and schools attended.

253. U.S. War Department, General Staff, G-2. *Japanese Defense Against Amphibious Operations.* Washington: Government Printing Office, 1945. 122 pp. PCarlMH

254. _____. *Japanese Military Installations.* n.p.: n.d. PCarlMH
Illustrated with photographs and maps.

255. _____. *Japanese Warfare.* n.p.: 1942. 36 pp. PCarlMH
Provides description of troops, equipment and activities.

256. _____. *Japanese Warfare, A Summary.* n.p.: 1942. PCarlMH

257. _____. *Photo Interpreter's Guide to Japanese Military Installations.* n.p.: 1945. PCarlMH
Strong emphasis on buildings and fortifications found in Central Pacific islands.

258. U.S. War Department, Military Intelligence Service. *Japanese Warfare: A Summary.* Washington: Government Printing Office, 1942. 84 pp. (Information Bulletin No. 16. "Restricted") DLC

259. _____. *Soldier's Guide to the Japanese Army.* Washington: Government Printing Office, 182 pp. (Special Series No. 27) DLC

260. Van Der Rhoer, Edward. *Deadly Magic, a Personal Account of Communications Intelligence in World War II in the Pacific.* New York: Charles Scribners and Sons, 1978. 225 pp. DLC
Author served with naval communications intelligence during the war.

261. Vanderveen, Bart H. *The Observer's Fighting Vehicle Directory. World War II.* New York: Frederick Warne & Co., 1969. 340 pp. DLC
Excellent review and photographs of the various vehicles used by combatants during WWII, arranged by country and vehicle type.

262. Vatcher, William H., Jr. "Combat Propaganda Against Japan in the Central Pacific." unpublished Doctoral Thesis, Stanford Univ., 1950. CSt-V

263. *The War Against Japan, Pictorial Record.* Washington: Office of the Chief of Military History [Government Printing Office], 1952. 471 pp. (United States Army in World War II, Pictorial Record) PCarlMH
Collection of U.S. Army photographs, indexed by subject.

264. Warner, Philip. *Japanese Army of World War II.* New York: Hippocrene Books, 1973. 40 pp. PCarlMH
General review.

265. Weigley, Russell F. *History of the United States Army.* New York: Macmillan Pub. Co., 1967. 668 pp. PCarlMH
Comprehensive history including a brief review of the Central Pacific campaign.

GENERAL HISTORIES   37

266. Wheeler, Keith. *Japan at War*. Alexandria, VA: Time-Life Books, 1982. 208 pp. DLC
Excellent pictorial history of the Japanese operations during the War.

267. _____ *Bombers over Japan*. Alexandria, VA: Time-Life Books, 1982. 208 pp. DLC
Excellent pictorial history of the bomber offensive over Japan, with much concerning the Marianas bases.

268. Wheeler, Richard. *A Special Valor, the U.S. Marines and the Pacific War*. New York: Harper & Row Pubs., 1983. 466 pp. DN
Single volume history of the Marines in the War for the general reader.

269. Wiley, Bell I. *The Building and Training of Infantry Divisions*. Washington: Army Ground Forces, 1946. 65 pp. (Study no. 12) DLC
Provides useful background on the development and training of infantry divisions for the various theaters.

270. Williams, Mary H. *Chronology, 1941-1945*. Washington: Office of the Chief of Military History [Government Printing Office], 1960. 660 pp. (U.S. Army in World War II, Special Studies). PCarlMH
Chronology of events and actions with emphasis on army and army air force operations.

271. Williams, R. C., Jr. "Jap Defensive Tactics--Attu to Okinawa." *Infantry Journal*, LVII (Aug. 1945), pp. 28-32. PCarlMH
Review of the tactics used by the Japanese including those noted in the Central Pacific.

272. Willoughby, Malcolm F. *The U.S. Coast Guard in World War II*. Annapolis, MD: Naval Institute Press, 1957. 347 pp. DN
Review of Coast Guard participation including service in the Central Pacific Campaigns.

273. Winton, John. *War in the Pacific. Pearl Harbor to Tokyo Bay*. New York: Mayflower Books, 1978. 193 pp. DLC
Pictorial history.

274. Wylie, Joseph C. "Reflections on the War in the Pacific." *United States Naval Institute Proceedings*, LXXVIII (Apr. 1952), pp. 351-361. DN
Review of the strategic considerations in the Pacific War.

AIR OPERATIONS

275. Air Intelligence Group, Office of the Chief of Naval Operations. "Air War Against Japan, April 1944-August 1945." unpublished paper: Deputy Chief of Naval Operations (Air), 1944-45. 200 pp. DN
Bimonthly intelligence summaries.

38 THE CENTRAL PACIFIC CAMPAIGN, 1943-1944

276. Anderson, David A. B-29 Superfortress at War. New York: Charles Scribner's Sons, 1978. 176 pp. DLC
General history of the aircraft and its employment.

277. Anderson, Orvil A. "Air War in the Pacific." Airpower Historian, IV (Oct. 1957), pp. 216-227.
Review of the role of the Army Air Force units in the Pacific Theater.

278. Blassingame, Wyatt. The Navy's Fliers in World War II. Philadelphia: Westminister Press, 1967. 258 pp. DN

279. Buchanan, A. R., editor. The Navy's Air War: A Mission Completed. New York: Harper, 1946. 432 pp. DLC
General history of the naval and marine aviation in World War II.

280. Caiden, Martin. Golden Wings: A Pictorial History of the United States Navy and Marine Corps in the Air. New York: Random House, 1960. 232 pp. DN
General pictorial history of naval and marine aviation, including their activities in World War II.

281. Camouflage & Markings No. 19: Boeing B-29 Superfortress, USAAF, 1942-1945. London: Ducimus Books, n.d. pp.146-167. DLC
Pictorial review, providing an excellent review of the aircraft markings including those that were based in the Marianas Islands.

282. Carter, Kit C., and Robert Mueller. The Army Air Forces in World War II, Combat Chronology, 1941-1945. Washington: Government Printing Office, 1973. 991 pp. PCarlMH
Last volume of the official history series, provides a comprehensive daily chronology by theater.

283. Cate, James L., and Wesley F. Craven, editors. The Army Air Force in World War II. Vol. IV. The Pacific: Guadalcanal to Saipan, August 1942 to July 1944. Chicago: Univ. of Chicago Press, 1950. 825 pp. PCarlMH
Official history providing a comprehensive review of its activities in the Pacific Theaters.

284. _____. The Army Air Force in World War II. Vol. VII, Services Around the World. Chicago: Univ. of Chicago Press, 1958. 667 pp. PCarlMH
Official history concerns the service forces and supply overseas.

285. Christy, Joe, editor. WWII: US Navy & Japanese Combat Planes. Blue Ridge Summit, PA: Tab Books, 1981. 159 pp. DLC
Review of the various aircraft used in the Pacific during WWII.

286. DuPre, Flint O. U.S. Air Force Biographical Dictionary. New York: Franklin Watts, 1965. 273 pp. DLC
Alphabetical listing of brief biographical sketches of noted Air Force officers including Medal of Honor winners.

GENERAL HISTORIES 39

287. Fabyanic, Thomas A. Strategic Air Attack in the United States Air Force: A Case Study. Manhattan, KS: Military Affairs/Aerospace Historian, n.d. 206 pp. DLC
Includes a detailed account of strategic air operations in the Pacific during the war.

288. Francillon, Rene J. Japanese Aircraft of the Pacific War. Annapolis: Naval Institute Press, 1987. 570 pp. DN
Comprehensive review of the various Japanese aircraft, including photographs and line drawings.

289. _____ U.S. Army Air Forces in the Pacific. Fallbrook, CA: Aero Pubs., 1969. 96 pp. DLC
Pictorial history of the Army Air Forces with attention given to aircraft markings and colorings.

290. General View of Japanese Military Aircraft in the Pacific War. Tokyo: Kantosha Co., 1956. 2 vols.
Comprehensive review of Japanese aircraft by the staff of Airview.

291. Goodman, Warren H. "Marine Corps Aviation in World War II: December 7, 1941-December 7, 1944." unpublished paper: U.S.M.C. File, Naval History Division, Operational Archives, n.d. 15 pp.
Brief review of Marine Air activities in the Pacific.

292. _____ "One Job-One Corps." Marine Corps Gazette, XXVIII (Nov. 1944), pp. 22-24. DN
Review of Marine air support concepts of Marine ground units.

293. Hansel, Haywood S., Jr. Offensive Air Operations against Japan. n.p.: 1953. 51 pp.
Author served on LeMay's staff.

294. _____ Strategic Air War Against Japan. Maxwell Air Force Base, AL: Airpower Research Institute, Air War College, 1983. 151 pp. DLC
Comprehensive account of air campaigns in the Pacific.

295. Haugland, Vern. The AAF Against Japan. New York: Harper, 1948. 515 pp. DLC
General review of the war by a wartime correspondent with the AAF.

296. Herbert, Kevin. Maximum Effort: The B-29s Against Japan. Manhattan, KS: Sunflower Univ. Press, 1983. 102 pp. DLC
Written from B-29 crew member's perspective.

297. Hopkins, George E. "Bombing and the American Conscience during World War II." Historian, XXVIII (May 1966), pp. 451-473.
Review of public reaction to bombing of German and Japanese cities.

298. Horikoshi, Jiro. Eagles of Mitsubishi: The Story of the Zero Fighter. Translated by Shorjiro Shindo and Harold N. Wantiez. Seattle: Univ. of Washington Press, 1981. 176 pp. DLC
Review of Japan's wartime standard fighter aircraft by its chief designer.

299. Hubler, Richard G., and John A. DeChant. <u>Flying Leathernecks: The Complete Record of Marine Corps Aviation in Action, 1941-1944.</u> Garden City: Doubleday, Doran, 1944. 225 pp. DN
Review of Marine aviation in the Pacific, of limited usefulness due to wartime censorship.

300. Jablonski, Edward. <u>Airwar.</u> Garden City, NY: Doubleday & Co., 1971. 2 vols. DLC
Pictorial history of air operations during WWII including the Pacific operations.

301. Kennett, Lee. <u>A History of Strategic Bombing.</u> New York: Charles Scribner's Sons, 1983. 222 pp. DLC
Broad review of strategic bombing including the bombing of Japanese cities.

302. Larkins, William T. <u>U.S. Marine Corps Aircraft, 1914-1959.</u> Concord, CA: Aviation History Pub., 1959. 125 pp. DLC
Pictorial review with aircraft specifications, performance, and limited service history provided for each aircraft.

303. LeMay, Curtis E., and Bill Yenne. <u>Superfortress: The Story of the B-29 and American Airpower.</u> New York: McGraw-Hill Book Co., 1988. 222 pp. DLC
Excellant account of air considerations involved with Central Pacific Campaign and the strategic bombing operations against the Japanese homeland.

304. Lindley, John W. <u>The Air War in the Pacific, Carrier Victory.</u> New York: Elsevier-Dutton, 1978. 184 pp. DLC
Review of naval air operations for the general reader.

305. MacIsaac, David. <u>Strategic Bombing in World War II: The Story of the United States Strategic Bombing Survey.</u> New York: Garland Pub., 1976. 231 pp. DLC
Review of the background and accomplishments of the Strategic Bombing Survey conducted after WWII. See entries 247-249, 603, 757, 775.

306. Matt, Paul R., comp. <u>United States Navy and Marine Corps Fighters, 1918-1962.</u> Bruce Robertson, editor. Los Angeles: Aero Pubs., 1962. 94 pp. DLC
Pictorial history and review of development and deployment of marine and naval aircraft.

307. McJennett, John. "Air Power for Ground Support." <u>Marine Corps Gazette</u>, XXIX (Aug. 1945), pp. 15-16+. DN
Review of effectiveness of air support for ground operations up to Okinawa.

308. McKay, Ernest A. <u>Carrier Strike Force. Pacific Air Combat in World War II.</u> New York: Messner, 1981. DLC
General account of operations.

GENERAL HISTORIES   41

309. Mingos, Howard. *American Heroes of the War in the Air*. New York: Lancair Pubs., 1943. 557 pp.   DLC
Brief history of the air war up to late 1943 and the citations of aviators of the various services including the Marines.

310. Monday, David. *USAAF at War in the Pacific*. New York: Scribners, 1980. 160 pp.   DLC
Pictorial history.

311. Murphy, Charles J. V. "The Air War on Japan." *Fortune*, XXXII (Sept. 1945), pp. 117-123;   (Oct. 1945), pp. 132-137+.   DLC
Review of the development and operations of the strategic bombing campaigns against Japan.

312. "Navy Wings Over the Pacific." *National Geographic*, LXXXVI (Aug. 1944), pp. 241-248.   DLC
Photographic review of naval airpower.

313. Okumiyu, Masatake, and Jiro Horikoshi, with Martin Caiden. *Zero! The Story of the Japanese Navy Air Force*. London: Cassell, 1957. 364 pp.   DN
Excellent review of the issues and problems that faced the Japanese Navy Air Force during the war.

314. Pratt, Fletcher. *The Navy Has Wings*. New York: Harper, 1943. 224 pp.   DN
One of the best histories written during the war concerning early WWII Naval Aviation.

315. Rosignoli, Guido. *Air Force Badges and Insignia of World War II*. New York: Arco Pub. Co., 1976. 200 pp.   DLC
Includes color plates of unit and rank insignia arranged by country.

316. Sakai, Saburo, with Martin Caidin and Fred Saito. *Samurai!* New York: E. P. Dutton, 1957. 382 pp.   DN
Excellent account of Japanese naval aviation by one of Japan's leading wartime aces.

317. Sherrod, Robert L. *History of Marine Corps Aviation in World War II*. Washington: Combat Forces Press, 1952. 496 pp.   DN
Excellent account of the role of Marine aviation in WWII. Includes a brief history of every marine aviation unit active during the war.

318. Sherry, Michael S. *The Rise of American Air Power: The Creation of Armageddon*. New Haven: Yale Univ. Press, 1987. 435 pp.   DLC
Comprehensive review of strategic bombing including the decisions that led up to the bombing of Japanese cities.

319. Sims, Edward H. *Greatest Fighter Missions of Top Navy and Marine Aces of World War II*. New York: Harper, 1962. 250 pp.   DLC

320. Sullivan, W. E., Jr. "The History and Development of Close Air Support." *Marine Corps Gazette*, XL (Nov. 1956), pp. 20-24.   DN
Review of Marine close air support, including Saipan.

321. Sunderland, James F., editor. World War II in the Air: The Pacific. New York: F. Watts, 1962. 2 vols. DLC
Collection of mostly reprinted articles concerning the American air effort for the general reader.

322. Swanborough, Gordon, and Peter M. Bowers. United States Navy Aircraft since 1911. New York: Funk & Wagnalls, 1968. 518 pp. DLC
Brief history and line drawing of every naval aircraft used in the Pacific War.

323. _____. United States Military Aircraft since 1909. New York: Putnam, 1963. 596 pp. DLC
Brief history and line drawing of every army aircraft used in the Pacific War.

324. Thorpe, Donald W. Japanese Army Air Force Camouflage and Markings, World War II. Fallsbrook, CA: Aero Pubs., 1968. 202 pp. DLC
Comprehensive pictorial review of aircraft markings, heavily illustrated with color plates.

325. _____. Japanese Naval Air Force Camouflage and Markings, World War II. Fallsbrook, CA: Aero Pubs., 1977. 192 pp. DLC
Companion volume to above concerning the naval aircraft.

326. U.S. Army, Office of the Chief of Military History. Japanese Monographs and Japanese Studies on Manchuria. Washington: Office of the Chief of Military History, 1945-1960.

> No. 124. Homeland Defense Naval Operations, Part III, June 1944-August 1945. 58 pp.
> Japanese reactions to the B-29 raids and retaliatory raids on the Marianas Islands.
> No. 157. Homeland Air Defense Operations Record (revised) July 1944-August 1945. 167 pp.
> Review of the Japanese Air organization and reactions to the B-29 raids.

327. U.S. Army Air Forces. Official Guide to the Army's Air Forces: A Directory, Almanac, and Chronicle of Achievement. New York: Simons, 1944. 380 pp. PCarlMH
Brief review of the Army Air Forces up to 1944.

328. U.S. Army Air Force, Historical Office. Army Air Forces in the War Against Japan, 1941-1942. Washington: HQ, Army Air Forces, 1945. 171 pp. PCarlMH
Review of early operations in the Pacific.

329. U.S. Navy, Office of the Deputy of Naval Operations (Air). "Air Task Organization in Pacific Ocean Areas: Task Organization of Land-based Aircraft." unpublished paper: n.d. 352 pp. DN
Review of naval land-based air organizations by geographic area.

330. U.S. Navy, Pacific Fleet and Pacific Ocean Area. Supplement No. 1 to Special Translation No. 20--Data on Japanese Naval Air Groups. n.p.: 1945. (CincPac-CincPoa Bulletin No. 25-45) DN

331. U.S. Navy, Naval History Division. U.S. Naval Aviation in the Pacific. Washington: Government Printing Office, 1947. 56 pp. DN
General review of the role that naval air played during the War.

332. Whitehouse, Arch. Squadrons of the Sea. Garden City, NY: Doubleday, 1962. 383 pp. DLC
Review of naval aviation including World War II and the Pacific Campaigns.

NAVAL OPERATIONS

333. Andreieu d'Albas, Emmanual. Death of a Navy: Japanese Naval Action in World War II. New York: Devin-Adair, 1957. 362 pp. DN
One of the early postwar histories of Japanese Naval Operations.

334. Angas, W. Mack. "Seagoing Navy Yard follows the Fleet..." Popular Science, CXXXVII (Nov. 1945), pp. 121-124. DLC
Excellent account concerning the mobility of the seagoing dry docks.

335. Ballantine, Duncan S. U.S. Naval Logistics in the Second World War. Princeton, NJ: Princeton Univ. Press, 1947. 308 pp. DN
Excellent study on the impact of logistics on the operations in the Pacific War.

336. Battle Stations! Your Navy in Action: A Photographic Epic of the Naval Operations of World War II... New York: William H. Wise, 1946. 402 pp. DN
Early pictorial history of the USN, USMC, and USCG operations during the war. Photographs lack detail of later histories.

337. Belote, James H., and William M. Titans of the Seas: The Development and Operations of Japanese and American Carrier Task Forces during World War II. New York: Harper & Row, 1975. 336 pp. DLC
General account of the carrier operations in the Pacific.

338. Best, Herbert. The Webfoot Warriors: The Story of UDT, the Navy's Underwater Demolition Teams. New York: John Day, 1962. 187 pp. DLC
Popular account of the activities of the Navy underwater demolition teams.

339. Blair, Clay, Jr. Silent Victory. The U.S. Submarine War Against Japan. New York: Lippincott, 1975. 1072 pp. DLC
Considered the best account of American submarine warfare in WWII.

340. Carter, Worrall R. Beans, Bullets, and Black Oil. The Story of Fleet Logistics Afloat in the Pacific during World War II. Washington: Government Printing Office, 1953. 482 pp. DLC
Excellent history of fleet logistic forces during the Pacific War and the Central Pacific campaigns.

341. Dull, Paul S. A Battle History of the Imperial Japanese Navy, 1941-1945. Annapolis: Naval Institute Press, 1978. 402 pp. DN
Excellent review of the Japanese viewpoint of the naval aspects of the Pacific War.

342. Ellis, Chris. United States Navy Warship Camouflage, 1939-1945. London: Johel Print. Services, 1975. 52 pp. DLC
Reference guide to colors and schemes applied to US warships during the World War II period.

343. Evans, David C., editor. The Japanese Navy in World War II. In the Words of Former Japanese Naval Officers. 2nd Edition. Annapolis: Naval Institute Press, 1986. 400 pp. DN
Seventeen essays concerning strategy, tactics, operations and leaders.

344. Fahey, James C. The Ships and Aircraft of the United States Fleet. War Edition. New York: Ships and Aircraft, 1942. 64 pp.
One of the standard references available to the public during the war, contains limited photos and ship and aircraft data.

345. Fane, Francis D., and Don Moore. The Naked Warriors. New York: D. Appleton Century-Crofts, 1956. 308 pp. DN
Popular history of the Navy's underwater demolition teams.

346. Furer, Julius A. Administration of the Navy Department in World War II. Washington: Government Printing Office, 1959. DN
Excellent administrative history of the Navy during the war.

347. Gallagher, Barrett. Flattop. Garden City, NY: Doubelday, 1959. 126 pp. DLC
Popular history including Central Pacific operations.

348. Genda, Minoru. "Tactical Planning in the Imperial Japanese Navy." Naval War College Review, XXII (Oct. 1969), pp. 45-50. DN
Review of the changing tactical concepts from focusing on battleships to carrier aviation.

349. Grosvenor, Melvin B. "Landing Craft for Invasion." National Geographic, LXXXVI (July 1944), pp. 1-30. DLC
Photographic review of types and deployment of the various types of landing craft used.

350. Hessler, William H. "The Carrier Task Force in World War II." United States Naval Institute Proceedings, LXXI (Nov. 1945), pp. 1271-1281. DN
Review the development and deployment of the carrier task forces.

GENERAL HISTORIES 45

351. Higgins, Edward T., and W. Dean Phillips. <u>Webfoot Warriors: The Story of a "Frogman" in the Navy during World War II</u>. New York: Exposition Press, 1955. 172 pp. DN
Personal narrative.

352. _____. <u>Undersea Victory: The Influence of Submarine Operations on the War in the Pacific</u>. Garden City, NY: Doubleday, 1966. 505 pp. DLC
Popular history for general reader.

353. Howarth, Stephen. <u>The Fighting Ships of the Rising Sun: The Drama of the Imperial Japanese Navy, 1895-1945</u>. New York: Atheneum, 1983, 398 pp. DLC
Popular history stressing the development of ship designs.

354. Hoyt, Edwin P. <u>The Carrier War</u>. New York: Lancer Books, 1972. 176 pp. (Lancer's Photobook History of Modern Combat, No. 6) DN
General photographic history.

355. _____. <u>How They Won the War in the Pacific: Nimitz and His Admirals</u>. New York: Weybright and Talley, 1970. 554 pp. DN
Review of the command relationships and personalities of the naval command in the Pacific.

356. Ito, Masanori. <u>The End of the Imperial Japanese Navy</u>. Translated by Andrew Y. Kuroda and Roger Pineau. New York: Norton, 1967. 240 pp. DN
General account of the Japanese perspective of the naval war in the Pacific.

357. <u>Jane's Fighting Ships</u>. London: Sampson, Low, Marston Co., 1939-1945. [published annually] DN
Best reference available concerning ship specifications, includes photograph and line drawing of each class of ships, arranged by country and class of ships. Pre and post-war editions are best for WWII ship information since the wartime editions were subject to censorship.

358. Jensen, Oliver O. <u>The Carrier War</u>. New York: Simon and Schuster, 1945. 172 pp. DN
Photographic history of the fast carrier operations in the Pacific.

359. King, Ernest J. <u>The United States Navy at War, 1941-1945. Official Reports to the Secretary of the Navy</u>. Washington: Government Printing Office, 1946. 305 pp. DN
Excellent summaries of the official reports by the Chief of Naval Operations with much concerning the Central Pacific campaigns.

360. Lockwood, Charles A., and Hans Christian Adamson. <u>Hellcats of the Sea</u>. New York: Greenberg, 1955. 335 pp. DN
Review of submarine warfare by the Pacific Submarine Force Commander.

46 THE CENTRAL PACIFIC CAMPAIGN, 1943-1944

361. _____. *Zoomies, Subs, and Zeros*. New York: Greenberg, 1956. 301 pp. DN
Submarine "lifeguard" operations in rescuing pilots.

362. Lott, Arnold S. "Japan's Nightmare - Mine Blockade." *United States Naval Institute Proceedings*, LXXXV (Nov. 1959), pp. 39-51. DN
Review of the mining of Japanese waters including the impact of the Central Pacific campaigns.

363. Macintyre, Donald F. G. W. *Aircraft Carrier: The Majestic Weapon*. New York: Ballantine Books, 1972. 160 pp. (Ballantine's Illustrated History of World War II)
Pictorial history of the aircraft carrier in World War II.

364. Mathews, Edward J. "What Ship's That." *United States Naval Institute Proceedings*, LIV (July 1978), pp. 61-73 pp. DN
Review of the Identification and Characteristics Section, Naval Intelligence Division operations during the war.

365. Meigs, John F. "Japanese Sea Power." *United States Naval Institute Proceedings*, LXX (Feb. 1944), pp. 121-129. DN
Review of the naval war suffers from wartime censorship.

366. Mickle, Peter, and others. *Warships of the Imperial Japanese Navy, 1895-1945*. Annapolis, MD: Naval Institute Press, 1977. 284 pp. DLC
Comprehensive study of Japanese warship design.

367. Miller, Max. *Daybreak for Our Carrier*. New York: Whittlesey House, McGraw-Hill, 1944. 184 pp. DN
Pictorial review of an unidentified American carrier in the Pacific War.

368. _____. *It's Tomorrow Out Here*. New York: Dodd, Mead, 1945. 186 pp.
Photographic history of the Naval War in the Pacific.

369. Miller, Vernon J. "Major Fleet Units Lost during World War II." *United States Naval Institute*, LXXXV (Jan. 1960), pp. 90-101. DN
Useful compilation by country of major ships lost during the war.

370. Moreel, Ben. "The SeaBees in World War II." *United States Naval Institute Proceedings*, LXXXVI (Mar. 1962), pp. 85-101 DN
Pictorial history.

371. Morrison, Samuel E. *The Two Ocean War: A Short History of the United States Navy in the Second World War*. Boston: Little, Brown and Co., 1963. 611 pp. DN
Abridged edition of the 15 volume series. Very readable and comprehensive.

GENERAL HISTORIES   47

372. Nimitz, Chester W., and others. *Triumph in the Pacific: The Navy's Struggle Against Japan*. Englewood Cliffs, NJ: Prentice-Hall, 1963. 186 pp. DN
Review of the Naval War against Japan with commentary on the various operations.

373. "Nimitz' Navy." *Life*, XVI (Mar. 6, 1944), pp. 41-44. DLC
Photographic review with commentary on Japan's reaction to the fall of the Marianas.

374. O'Connor, Raymond G., editor. *The Japanese Navy in World War II*. Annapolis: Naval Institute Press, 1969. 147 pp. DN
Collection of essays written by Japanese officers.

375. "Our Submarine Victory in the Pacific." *United States Naval Institute Proceedings*, LXXIV (Sept. 1948), pp. 1147-1155. DN
Pictorial review.

376. Poling, James. *All Battle Stations Manned: The U.S. Navy in World War II*. New York: Grosset & Dunlap, 1971. 249 pp. DLC
General history.

377. Possony, Stafan T. "Japanese Naval Strategy." *United States Naval Institute Proceedings*. LXX (May 1944), pp. 515-524. DN
Review of the Japanese war strategy.

378. Potter, Elmer B. "The Japanese Navy Tells Its Story." *United States Naval Institute Proceedings*, LXXIII (Feb. 1947), pp. 137-143. DN
Abridged edition of *Interrogations of Japanese Officials*, see No. 248.

379. _____. "The Navy's War Against Japan--A Strategic Analysis." *United States Naval Institute Proceedings*, LXXVI (Aug. 1950), pp. 824-837. DN
Excellent review of the naval war in the Pacific.

380. Pratt, Fletcher. *Fleet Against Japan*. New York: Harper, 1946. 263 pp. DN
General history of the Naval War in the Pacific.

381. Reg, Ingraham. *First Fleet: The Story of the U.S. Coast Guard at War*. New York: Bobbs-Merrill Co., 1944. 310 pp. DN
Brief history by a *Time* magazine correspondent including brief references to early Central Pacific operations.

382. Reynolds, Clark G. *The Carrier War*. Alexandria, VA: Time-Life Books, 1982. 176 pp. DN
Popular history and pictorial of WWII in the Pacific

383. _____. *The Fast Carriers: The Forging of an Air Navy*. New York: McGraw-Hill Book Co., 1968. 498 pp. DN
Considered the best overall treatment of the development and employment of the Navy's fast carriers.

384. _____ "History and Development of the Fast Carrier Task Forces, 1943-1945." PhD Dissertation, Duke Univ., 1964.

385. Roland, Charles. Troopships of World War II. Washington: Army Transportation Assn., 1947. 374 pp. DLC
Pictorial review of Army troopships.

386. Roscoe, Theodore. On the Seas and in the Skies: A History of the U.S. Navy's Air Power. New York: Hawthorne Books, 1970. DN
Comprehensive review of naval air operations including the Pacific campaigns.

387. _____ United States Destroyer Operations in World War II. Annapolis: Naval Institute Press, 1953. 581 pp. DN
Compilation of stories concerning destroyers, including support activities in the Central Pacific.

388. _____ United States Submarine Operations in World War II. Annapolis: Naval Institute Press, 1949. 577 pp. DN
Compilation of stories concerning submarines, including support activities in the Central Pacific.

389. Schoun, Karl. U.S. Navy Biographical Dictionary. New York: Franklin Watts, 1964. 277 pp. DN
Biographical sketches of famous naval officers including many from the WWII period and Medal of Honor winners.

390. Sears, Stephan W. Carrier War in the Pacific. New York: American Heritage, 1966. 153 pp. (American Heritage Junior Library). DLC
Account of the fast carrier task forces for young readers.

391. Smith, S. E., editor. The United States Navy in World War II. New York: William Morrow, 1986. 1049 pp. DLC
Popular history of the naval war.

392. Steichen, Edward, comp. Power in the Pacific, a Pictorial Record of Navy Combat Operations on Land, Sea, and the Sky. New York: U.S. Camera Pub. Co., 1945. 144 pp.
Compilation of mostly USN official photos with captions.

393. _____ U.S. Navy War Photographs: Pearl Harbor to Tokyo Bay. New York: U.S. Camera, 1946. 108 pp. DN
Excellent compilation of official USN photographs.

394. Stephenson, Hal W. Analysis of Battle Statistics for the Pacific Islands in World War II. 2nd Edition. Bennington, VT: Weapons and Warfare Press, 1984. 22 pp.
Compilation of statistics concerning force ratios, casualties, battle dead, loss ratios, length of battles.

GENERAL HISTORIES 49

395. U.S. Army, Far East Command. The Imperial Japanese Navy in World War II. A Graphic Presentation of the Japanese Naval Organization and List of Combatants and Non-combatants Vessels Lost or Damaged in the War. Tokyo: Military History Section, Far East Command, 1952. 279 pp. (Japanese Monograph No. 116) DN
One of the better early reviews of the Japanese Navy.

396. _____ Operational History of Naval Communications (December 1941-August 1945). Edited Translation. Washington: U.S. Army Japanese Research Division, n.d. 407 pp. (Japanese Monograph No. 118) CMH
Comprehensive review of Japanese communications, cryptography, and radar developments.

397. _____ Outline of Third Phase Operations (February 1943-August 1945. Unedited translation. Washington: U.S. Army Japanese Research Division, n.d. 44 pp. (Japanese Monograph No. 117) CMH
General review of Japanese naval operations from the fall of Guadalcanal to the end of the War.

398. _____ Surface Escort Operations (December 1941-August 1945). Tokyo: Military History Section, Far East Command, n.d. 16 pp. (Japanese Monograph No. 125) CMH
Review of Shipping Command Headquarters organizations and plans.

399. "A U.S. Carrier fights an Airplane Fire." Life, XVII, (Dec. 4, 1944), pp. 62-64. DLC
Interesting pictorial review of the damage control and rescue operations used on the large carriers.

400. U.S. Coast Guard, Public Information Division, Historical Section. The Coast Guard at War, Volume VI, The Pacific Landings. Washington: Historical Section, Public Information Section, U.S.C.G., 1946. 292 pp. DN
Compilation of official reports and statistics.

401. U.S. Coast Guard, Public Relations Division. United States Coast Guard. Combat and Overseas Operations. Washington: Public Relations Division, U.S.C.G., 1945. 77 pp. DN
Chronology of Coast Guard operations, including those in the Central Pacific.

402. U.S. Joint Army-Navy Assessment Committee. Japanese Naval and Merchant Shipping Losses during World War II by All Causes. Washington: Government Print. Office, 1947. DLC
Excellent summation and listing of Japanese shipping losses.

403. U.S. Navy, Bureau of Naval Personnel. Register of Commissioned and Warrant Officers of the United States Navy and Marine Corps on Active Duty. Washington: Government Printing Office, 1941-1945. DLC
Published annually, provides birth date, schools attended and when ranks obtained for each officer.

404. U.S. Navy, Commander in Chief, Pacific Fleet. "Administrative History of the Forward Area, Central Pacific and the Marianas Area." unpublished paper: 1946. 194 pp. DN
Administrative history of the Headquarters activites in administrating the Gilbert, Marshall, and Marianas Islands groups as well as Iwo Jima and the Ellice Islands.

405. _____. "Administrative History of Minecraft Pacific Fleet." unpublished paper: 1946. 215 pp. DN
Comprehensive review of mine warfare and minecraft commands.

406. _____. "Commander in Chief, United States Pacific Fleet and Pacific Ocean Areas, Command History." unpublished paper, 1946. 3 vols. DN
Administrative history of the naval war in the Pacific.

407. _____. "History of the Amphibious Forces, U.S. Pacific Fleet." unpublished paper: 1945. 4 vols. DN
Comprehensive review and history concerning the development and operations of amphibious doctrine.

408. _____. "History of Service Force, U.S. Pacific Fleet." unpublished paper: 1946. 389 pp. DN
Comprehensive review of the service and logistic forces of the Pacific Fleet.

409. U.S. Navy Historical Division. *United States Naval Chronology, World War II*. Washington: Government Printing Office, 1955. 214 pp. DN
Useful compilation of events emphasizing naval and marine operations.

410. U.S. Navy History Division. *Dictionary of American Naval Fighting Ships*. Washington: Government Printing Office, 1959-1981. 8 vols. DN
   Vol. 1. A-B, appendix concerning battleships, cruisers, destroyers, and submarines.
   2. C-F, appendix concerning aircraft carriers.
   3. G-K.
   4. L-M, appendix concerning amphibious ships.
   5. N-Q, appendix concerning minecraft.
   6. R-S.
   7. T-V, appendix concerning LST's.
   8. W-Z, guide to series.
Invaluable source for ship histories and specifications, arranged alphabetically by name of ship, appendices provide information arranged by ship type.

411. U.S. Navy, Pacific Fleet. "Report of Operations in the Pacific Ocean Areas." unpublished paper: Fleets, Feb. 1942-December 1945. ca3000 pp. DN
Month by month detailed narrative by the Pacific Fleet Commander. Includes tables, charts, and diagrams.

GENERAL HISTORIES   51

412. U.S. Navy, Pacific Fleet and Pacific Ocean Areas. "Unity of Command as it functioned in the Pacific Ocean Areas in World War II." unpublished paper: Admin. Hist. Appen. CinCPac/Poa Analytical Div. 9, n.d. 35 pp. DN
Traces the origin and development of CINCPOA as a Joint Command.

413. _____ "Command History, World War II, 7 December 1941-15 August 1945." unpublished paper: Fleets, 1946. 445 pp. DN
History of the operations and responsibilities of CINCPAC-CINCPOA including descriptions of the Planning, Operations, Logistics, Intelligence, Communications and Internal Administrations Sections.

414. _____ The Development of Japanese Seapower. n.p.: 1945. (CincPac-CincPoa Bulletin 93-45. DN

415. _____ Important Flag Officers of the Japanese Navy. n.p.: 1944. (CincPac-CincPoa Bulletin 70-43) DN
Brief biographies of the important Japanese flag officers.

416. _____ Register of Japanese Naval Officers. n.p.: 1945. (CincPac-CincPoa Bulletin 43-45) DN

417. U.S. Navy, Pacific Fleet and Pacific Ocean Areas, Communications Division. "History of CINCPAC/CINCPOA Communications Division, 7 December 1941-15 August 1945." unpublished paper: Admin. Hist. Appen. CinCPac/CinCPoa Analytical Div. 13-14, 23 Sept 1945. 500 pp. DN
Comprehensive review of role in the CINCPOA Command.

418. U.S. Navy, Pacific Fleet and Pacific Ocean Areas. Intelligence Section. "A History of the Combat Intelligence Section, Staff CinC Pacific Fleet from 7 December 1941-September 1945." unpublished paper: Admin. Hist. Appen. CinCpac/Poa Analytical Div. 15-17. n.d. 450 pp. DN
History of the Intelligence Section as well as the Pacific Fleet Radio Unit.

419. U.S. Navy, Pacific Fleet and Pacific Ocean Areas. Logistic Division. "Historical Data on Information, Fuel and Lubricants Section, Logistics Division, Joint Staff, CinCPoa." unpublished paper: Admin. Hist. Appen. CinCPac/CinCPoa Analytical Div. 22, n.d. 34 pp. DN
Brief history including personnel assigned, policy, includes petroleum-use forecast indicators and charts of actual amounts dispensed.

420. _____ "History of the Administrative and Statistical Section, Logistics Division." unpublished paper: Admin. Hist. Append. CinCPac/Poa Analytical Div. 18, 21 September 1945. ca100 pp. DN
Brief history of the Division and extensive appendices of reports, abstracted data, and equipment inventories.

421. _____ "History of the Transportation Section, Logistics Division." unpublished paper: Admin. Hist. Appen. CinCPac/Poa Analytical Div. 23, 16 Oct 1945. 60 pp. DN
Comprehensive history of operations.

422. U.S. Navy, Pacific Fleet and Pacific Ocean Area, Military Government Section. "CINCPAC--CINCPOA Command History, Military Government Section." unpublished paper: Admin. Hist. Appen. CincPac/Poa Analytical Div. 29-30, n.d. ca225 pp. DN
Review and chronological summary of the operations in the Marshalls and Marianas.

423. U.S. Navy, Pacific Fleet and Pacific Ocean Area, Operations Division. "History of Operations Division." unpublished paper: Admin. Hist. Appen. CincPac/Poa Analytical Div. 31, 8 Oct 1945. ca225 pp. DN
Summary of the eight sections making up the Operations Division.

424. U.S. Navy, Pacific Fleet and Pacific Ocean Area, Public Information Office. "History of CINCPAC Public Information." unpublished paper: Admin. Hist. Appen. CincPac/Poa Analytical Div. 42-43. n.d. 60 pp. DN
Review and comments concerning the problems dealing with the press under wartime conditions.

425. U.S. Navy, Pacific Fleet and Pacific Ocean Area, War Plans Division. "History of the War Plans Division during War World II." unpublished paper: Admin. Hist. Appen. CincPac/Poa Analytical Div. 40, 11 Oct 1945. 13 pp. DN
Brief history tracing its evolution from the Fleet Planning Agency to a Joint Command comprised of representatives from all the services.

426. U.S. Navy, Service Force, Pacific. "A History of the Advanced Base Section." unpublished paper: Type Commands, 1 Oct 1945. 125 pp. DN
History of the Service Force and its planning and organizing for Central Pacific Drive.

427. Y´Blood, William T. The Little Giants. U.S. Escort Carriers Against Japan. Annapolis, MD: Naval Institute Press, 1981. 257 pp. DN
Concise history based on after action reports and veteran interviews.

428. Yokoi, Toshiyuki. "Thoughts on Japan´s Naval Defeat." United States Naval Institute Proceedings, LXXXVI (Oct. 1960), pp. 68-69. DN
Comprehensive review of Japan´s defeat by former INJ officer.

4.
Memoirs and Biographies

General Henry H. Arnold

429. Arnold, H. H. Global Mission. New York: Harper, 1949. 626 pp. PCarlMH
Autobiography of Commander of Army Air Forces during WWII, a strong advocate of the Central Pacific drive.

430. Coffey, Thomas M. Hap, the Story of the U.S. Air Force and the Man Who Built It: General Henry H. Arnold. New York: Viking Press, 1982. 482 pp. DLC
Best biography concerning Arnold.

431. Dupre, Flint O. Hap Arnold: Architect of American Air Power. New York: Macmillan Co., 1972. 144 pp. PCarlMH
Popular biography.

Vice Admiral Arleigh Burke

432. Burke, Adm. Arleigh A. "An Evening with Admiral Burke." unpublished paper: Individual Personnel, 8 March 1968. 43 pp. DN
A discussion between Prof. Langdon, USNA, and Adm. Burke including World War II related subjects.

433. Jones, John K., and Hubert Kelley. Admiral Arleigh Burke: The Story of a Fighting Sailor. Philadelphia: Chilton Books, 1962. 203 pp. DN
Served as Admiral Spruance's Chief of Staff

Colonel Evans F. Carlson, USMC

434. Blankfort, Michael. *The Big Yankee: The Life of Carlson of the Raiders*. Boston: Little, Brown & Co., 1947. 380 pp. DN
Biography of Col. Evans F. Carlson, USMC, who served in varying capacities in the Gilbert through the Marianas campaign.

Vice Admiral Joseph "Jocko" Clark

435. Clark, Joseph J., and Clark G. Reynolds. *Carrier Admiral*. New York: McKay, 1967. 333 pp. DN
Considered Mitscher's most aggressive fast carrier task force commander.

Major General Charles H. Corlett

436. Corlett, Charles H. *Cowboy Pete: The Autobiography of Maj. Gen. Charles H. Corlett*. Edited by William Farkington. Sante Fe: Sleeping Fox Enterprises, 1974. 127 pp. PCarlMH
Commanded the 7th Infantry Division.

Brigadier General Pedro A. J. del Valle-Barca Munoz, USMC

437. del Valle-Barca Munoz, Pedro A. J. *Semper Fidelis: An Autobiography*. Hawthorne, CA: Christian Book Club, 1976. 187 pp. DLC
Commanded III Amphibious Corps Artillery during Guam operations.

Secretary of Navy James V. Forrestal

438. Forrestal, James V. *The Forrestal Diaries*. Edited by Walter Millis. New York: Viking Press, 1951. 581 pp. DLC
Useful for administrative aspects of the war.

439. Rogow, Arnold A. *Victim of Duty: A Study of James Forrestal*. London: Rupert Hart-Davis, 1966. 324 pp. DLC
Review of his career.

Major General Roy S. Geiger, USMC

440. Willock, Roger. *Unaccustomed to Fear: A Biography of General Roy S. Geiger, USMC*. Princeton, NJ: Privately Printed, 1968. 321 pp. DLC
Deputy Commander, I Marine Amphibious Corps, Senior Commander on shore at Guam.

MEMOIRS AND BIOGRAPHIES 55

Rear Admiral Cato D. Glover

441. Glover, Cato D. Command Performance--with Guts! New York: Greenwich Book Pub. co., 1969. 215 pp. DLC
Autobiographical account of experiences, including command of the USS Barnes, CVE-20, and as Head of the Pacific Planning Section, Plans Division of HQ, Commander in Chief.

Tameichi Hara, IJN

442. Hara, Tameichi. Japanese Destroyer Captain. New York: Ballantine Books, 1961. 311 p. PCarlMH
Memoirs of a Japanese destroyer captain's experiences during the war.

Emperor Hirohito

443. Mosley, Leonard. Hirohito: Emperor of Japan. Englewood Cliffs, NJ: Prentice-Hall, 1966. 371 pp. PCarlMH
Comprehensive biography of Japan's reigning wartime monarch.

Harry Hopkins

444. Adams, Henry H. Harry Hopkins. A Biography. New York: G. P. Putnams' Sons, 1977. 448 pp. DLC
Administrative Assistance to President Roosevelt.

Lt. General George C. Kenney

445. Falk, Stanley L. "General Kenney, the Indirect Approach, and the B-29's." Aerospace Historian, XXVII (Fall 1981), pp. 147-155. DN
Reviews opposition to Central Pacific deployment of B-29s.

446. Kenney, George C. General Kenney Reports. A Personal History of the Pacific War. New York: Duell, Sloan and Pearce, 1949. 549 pp. PCarlMH
MacArthur's air commander, advocated against the Central Pacific drive.

447. Wolk, Herman S. "The Other Founding Father." Air Force, MXX (Sept. 1987), pp. 164+. DLC
Provides an commentary on Gen. Kenney's views on the Central Pacific drive.

Admiral of the Fleet Ernest J. King

448. Buell, Thomas B. Master of Sea Power: A Biography of Fleet Admiral Ernest J. King. Boston: Little, Brown and Co., 1980. 609 pp. DN
Excellent biography of the Central Pacific strongest advocate.

449. King, Ernest J., and Walter M. Whitehill. <u>Fleet Admiral King, a Naval Record</u>. New York: Norton, 1952. 674 pp. DN
Autobiography of Commander-in-Chief, U.S. Fleet/Chief of Naval Operations, 1942-1945.

Admiral Mineichi Koga, IJN

450. U.S. Navy, Pacific Fleet and Pacific Ocean Area. <u>Biography of New Japanese Commander-in-Chief</u>. n.p.: 1944. (CincPac-CincPoa Bulletin 76-44)
Biography compiled by the Intelligence staff of the Pacific Fleet.

Rear Admiral Edwin T. Layton

451. Layton, Edwin T. <u>"And I Was There." Pearl Harbor and Midway-Breaking the Secrets</u>. New York: William Morrow & Co., 1985. 596 pp. DLC
Memoirs of an intelligence officer on Nimitz's staff.

Fleet Admiral William D. Leahy

452. Adams, Henry H. <u>Witness to Power, the Life of Fleet Admiral William D. Leahy</u>. Annapolis, MD: Naval Institute Press, 1985. 391 pp. DN
Provides a review of the British arguments for Europe vs. the Navy's Pacific priorities.

453. Leahy, William D. <u>I Was There: The Personal Story of the Chief of Staff to Presidents Roosevelt and Truman, Based on His Notes and Diaries Made at the Time</u>. New York: McGraw-Hill, 1950. 527 pp. DN
Chairman of the Joint Chiefs of Staff, 1942-1945.

General Curtis LeMay

454. Coffey, Thomas M. <u>Iron Eagle: The Turbulent Life of General Curtis LeMay</u>. New York: Crown Pubs., 1986. 474 pp. DLC
Popular biography including his World War II service in the Pacific.

455. LeMay, Curtis, with Mackinlay Kantor. <u>Mission with LeMay</u>. Garden City, NY: Doubleday & Co., 1965. 581 pp. DLC
Autobiography with emphasis on his command of 20th and 21st Bomb Commands, and the 20th Air Force during World War II.

Vice Admiral Charles Lockwood

456. Lockwood, Charles. <u>Sink 'em All. Submarine Warfare in the Pacific</u>. New York: Greenberg, 1955. 335 pp. DN
Memoirs of Pacific Fleet Submarine Force Commander.

MEMOIRS AND BIOGRAPHIES 57

General Douglas MacArthur

457. James, D. Clayton. The Years of MacArthur. Boston: Houghton Mifflin, 1970-1985. 3 vols. PCarlMH
Most complete biography of MacArthur; volume 2 covers the 1941-45 era.

458. Long, Gavin. MacArthur as Military Commander. Princeton, NJ: Van Nostrand, 1969. 243 pp. DLC
Provides background to the Philippine vs. the Central Pacific strategies.

459. MacArthur, Douglas. Reminiscences: General of the Army Douglas MacArthur. New York: McGraw-Hill Book Co., 1964. 438 pp. PCarlMH
Commanded the Allied forces in the Southwest Pacific Theater, advocated the Philippine approach to Japan rather than through the Central Pacific.

460. Manchester, William. American Caesar, Douglas MacArthur, 1880-1964. Boston: Little, Brown, and Co., 1978. 793 pp. PCarlMH
Balanced biography of the controversial general in the Pacific.

461. Mayer, Sydney L. MacArthur. New York: Ballantine Books, 1971. 160 pp. (Ballantine Illustrated History of World War II) DLC
Pictorial history with emphasis on World War II.

462. Whitney, Courtney. MacArthur: His Rendezvous with History. New York: Knopf, 1956. 547 pp. PCarlMH
Favorable biography by one his wartime staff officers.

463. Willoughby, Charles A., and John Chamberlain. MacArthur, 1941-1945, Victory in the Pacific. New York: McGraw-Hill Book Co., 1954. 441 pp. PCarlMH
Favorable biography by one of his staff officers.

Pfc William Manchester, USMC

464. Manchester, William. Goodbye Darkness, a Memoir of the Pacific War. Boston: Little, Brown & Co., 1979. 401 pp. DLC
Author's experiences with 6th Marine Division.

General George C. Marshall

465. Faber, Harold. Soldier and Statesman. General George C. Marshall. New York: Ariel Books, 1964. 227 pp. DLC
General biography for young readers.

466. Fyre, William. Marshall: Citizen Soldier. New York: Bobbs-Merrill, 1947. 397 pp. PCarlMH
Popular biography.

58 THE CENTRAL PACIFIC CAMPAIGN, 1943-1944

467. _____. The Winning of the War in Europe and the Pacific. New York: Simon and Schuster, 1945. 123 pp. PCarlMH
Biennial Report of the Chief of Staff of the US Army, 1943-45; provides an overview of US War plans and strategy.

468. Pogue, Forrest. George C. Marshall: Organizer for Victory. New York: Viking Press, 1975. 683 pp. PCarlMH
Best biography of Marshall covering the War Years; provides much insight to the debates concerning the Pacific strategy.

Vice Admiral Marc Mitscher

469. Burke, Arleigh A. "Admiral Marc Mitscher: A Naval Aviator." United States Naval Institute Proceedings, CI (Apr. 1975), pp. 53-63. DN
Comprehensive biography by one of his wartime staff members.

470. Taylor, Theodore. The Magnificent Mitscher. New York: W. W. Norton & Co., 1954. 364 pp. DN
Wartime biography of the Commander of the Central Pacific Fast Carriers.

Fleet Admiral Chester W. Nimitz

471. Driskill, Frank A., and Dede W. Casad. Chester W. Nimitz, Admiral of the Hills. Austin, TX: Eakin Press, 1983. 298 pp.
Popular biography.

472. Joan of Arc, Sister. My Name is Nimitz. San Antonio: Standard Print. Co., 1948. 115 pp. DLC
Family history.

473. Potter, Elmer B. "Chester William Nimitz, 1885-1966." United States Naval Institute Proceedings, XCII (Jan. 1966), pp. 30-55. DN
Brief biography and tribute by the foremost Nimitz biographer.

474. _____. Nimitz. Annapolis: Naval Institute Press, 1976. DN
Excellent biography of the Commander of Allied Forces in the Pacific Ocean Area, which included the Central Pacific.

475. Pratt, Fletcher. "Nimitz and His Admirals." Harper's Magazine, CXC (Feb. 1945), pp. 209-217. DLC
Brief review of the naval leadership in the Pacific War.

476. Weddle, Robert S. "Texas to Tokyo Bay: Admiral Chester W. Nimitz." American History Illustrated, X (Aug. 1975), pp. 4-10. DLC
General biography.

MEMOIRS AND BIOGRAPHIES 59

Rear Admiral Arthur W. Radford

477. Jurika, Stephen M. Jr., editor. <u>From Pearl Harbor to Vietnam: The Memoirs of Admiral Arthur W. Radford</u>. Stanford: Hoover Institution Press, 1980. 476 pp. DLC
Commanded one of fast carrier task forces.

Franklin D. Roosevelt
President of the United States

478. Bishop, Jim. <u>FDR's Last Year, April 1944-April 1945</u>. New York: William Morrow & Co., 1974. 690 pp. DLC
Detailed account of Roosevelt's last year including a review of his perspective on the need for the Marianas capture.

479. Burns, James M. <u>Roosevelt: The Soldier of Freedom, 1940-1945</u>. New York: Harcourt Brace Jovanovich, 1970. 722 pp. DLC
Detailed biography touching on Central Pacific Campaigns.

480. Divine, Robert. <u>Roosevelt and World War II</u>. Baltimore: Johns Hopkins Press, 1969. 107 pp. PCarlMH
Commentary on foreign policy issues.

481. Matloff, Maurice. <u>Mr. Roosevelt's Three Wars: FDR as a War Leader</u>. Colorado: U.S.A.F. Academy, 1964. 21 pp. (Harmon Memorial Lecture No. 6) PCarlMH
Commentary on his involvement with the military and naval leadership.

482. Larrabee, Eric. <u>Commander in Chief. Franklin Delano Roosevelt, His Lieutenants & Their War</u>. New York: Harper & Row, 1987. 723 pp. DN
Detailed account of his relations with the American high command.

Vice Admiral Frederick C. Sherman

483. Sherman, Frederick C. <u>Combat Command: The American Aircraft Carriers in the Pacific War</u>. New York: Dutton, 1950. 427 pp. DN
Commanded U.S.S. Saratoga, CV2, during Gilberts Campaign.

Major General David M. Shoup, USMC

484. Shoup, David M. "Shoup of the Marines." <u>Life</u>, LII (Mar. 23, 1962), pp. 49-61. DLC
Commanded 2nd Marine Regiment on Tarawa.

Lt. General Holland M. Smith, USMC

485. Cooper, Norman V. "The Military Career of General Holland M. Smith, USMC." Ph.D. Dissertation, Univ. of Alabama, 1974. AMS

486. Smith, Holland M., and Percy Finch. Coral and Brass. New York: Scribner's Sons, 1949. 289 pp. DN
Autobiography of Gen. Smith, who commanded the amphibious operations at Tarawa, Makin, Kwajalein, Saipan, Tinian, and later Iwo Jima.

487. _____. "Howlin' Mad's Own Story: Excerpts from Coral and Brass." Saturday Evening Post, CCXXXI (Nov. 20, 1948), pp. 32-33+. DLC
Abridged version of the above entry.

Fleet Admiral Raymond A. Sprunce

488. Buell, Thomas B. The Quiet Warrior. Boston: Little, Brown Co., 1974. 486 pp. DLC
Biography of the fleet and amphibious forces commander of the Central Pacific amphibious operations during the Battle of the Philippine Sea.

489. Forrestel, E. P. Admiral Raymond A. Sprunce, USN, a Study in Command. Washington: Navy Department [Government Printing Office], 1966. 275 pp. DN
Author was on Sprunce's staff.

490. Pratt, Fletcher. "Sprunce, Picture of an Admiral." Harpers Magazine, CXCIII (Aug. 1946), pp. 144-157. DLC
Detailed account of Central Pacific operations.

Secretary of War Henry L. Stimson

491. Current, Richard N. Secretary Stimson: A Study in Statecraft. New Brunswick, NJ: Rutgers Univ. Press, 1954. 272 pp. DLC
Account of his role in foreign policy development.

492. Stimson, Henry L., and George Bundy. On Active Service in Peace and War. New York: Harper, 1948. 698 pp. DLC
Provides insight to inter-service relations and issues facing the army.

Admiral Felix B. Stump

493. Stump, Felix B. "An Evening with Adm. Felix B. Stump." unpublished paper: Individual Personnel, 1967. 32 pp. DN
Commanding officer of the USS Lexington, CV 16; contains his observations and experiences during WWII and his later career.

MEMOIRS AND BIOGRAPHIES 61

Rear Admiral Edwin J. Taylor, Jr.

494. Taylor, Edwin J., Jr. "Memoirs, 1941-1946." unpublished paper: Individual Personnel, 1946. 29 pp. DN
Served on the USS Alabama (BB-60) and the USS South Dakota (BB-57) during the Battle of the Philippine Sea.

Foreign Minister Shigenori Togo

495. Togo, Shigenori. The Cause of Japan. Translated by Fumihiko Togo and Ben Blareney. New York: Simon & Schuster, 1956. 372 pp. PCarlMH
War memoirs of Japan's Foreign Minister.

Premier Hideki Tojo

496. Browne, Courtney. Tojo: The Last Bonzai. New York: Holt, Reinhart and Winston, 1967. 260 pp. PCarlMH
Japan's Premier, resigned as a result of the fall of the Marianas.

497. Butow, Robert C., Tojo and the Coming of the War. Princeton, NJ: Princeton Univ. Press, 1961. 584 pp. PCarlMH
Pre-war biography of the Premier who led Japan into War.

Vice Admiral Richmond K. Turner

498. Dyer, George C. The Amphibians Came to Conquer: The Story of Admiral Richmond Kelly Turner. Washington: Government Printing Office, 1972. 2 vols. DN
Wartime biography including his participation in the development of the landing techniques. He commanded the assault forces during the landing phases of the Central Pacific invasions.

General Alexander A. Vandegrift, USMC

499. Vandegrift, A. A., as told to Robert B. Asprey. Once a Marine: The Memoirs of General A. A. Vandegrift, U.S.M.C. New York: Norton, 1964. 293 pp. DN
Autobiography of the Commandant of the Marine Corps from January 1944 through the end of the War.

Lieutenant General Albert C. Wedemeyer

500. Wedemeyer, Albert C. Wedemeyer Reports. New York: Henry Holt & Co., 1958. 497 pp. PCarlMH
War memoirs of War Planner, 1940-43; participated in formulation of Army Pacific War plans.

501. Wedemeyer, Albert C., and Keith E. Eiler. "Man Who Planned Victory: An Interview with Gen. Albert C. Wedemeyer." *American Heritage*, XXXIV (June 1983), pp. 36-47. DLC
Review of his participation in planning including the Central Pacific drives.

5.
Gilbert Islands Operations

GENERAL WORKS

502. "Amphibious Operation: The Story of Tarawa." <u>Leatherneck</u>, XXVII (Feb. 1944), pp. 23-33. DN
Pictorial review.

503. "The Attack on Tarawa, Some Eyewitness Accounts." <u>Marine Corps Gazette</u>, XXVIII (Jan. 1944), pp. 7-14. DN
Firsthand accounts with photographs.

504. Bailey, Seth. <u>Battle for Tarawa</u>. Derby, CT: Monarch Books, 1962. 155 pp. DLC
Popular history for general reader.

505. Baldwin, Hanson. <u>Battles Won and Lost. Great Campaigns of World War II</u>. New York: Harper & Row Pub., 1966. 523 pp. DLC
Review of eleven major campaigns of World War II, including Tarawa, by the Military Editor and Analyst of the New York Times.

506. _____ "The Bloody Epic that was Tarawa." <u>New York Times Magazine</u>, (Nov. 16-23, 1958), pp. 19-21+. DLC

507. "The Battle for Tarawa." <u>Newsweek</u>, XXII (Dec. 6, 1943), pp. 22-23. DLC
Brief account of battle.

508. "The Battle for Tarawa Atoll." <u>Illustrated London News</u>, CCIV (Jan. 8, 1944), pp. 44-45.

509. Brown, Richard G. "Tarawa: Lest We Forget." <u>Marine Corps Gazette</u>, LXIV (Nov. 1980), pp. 46-50. DN
Review of the battle.

510. Brugioni, Dino A. "Aerial Photographs, an Overlooked Resource." *Fortitudine*, XII (Spring 1983), pp. 12-17. DN
Detailed review of the photo intelligence using Tarawa as a case study.

511. Burns, Eugene. "Butch O'Hare's Last Fight." *Saturday Evening Post*, CCXVI (Mar. 11, 1944), pp. 19+. DLC
Medal of Honor winner carrier pilot shot down over Tarawa.

512. Cooley, Thomas J. "The Aerial Photo in Amphibious Intelligence." *Marine Corps Gazette*, XXVIII (Oct. 1945), pp. 32-35. DN
Review of the discussions concerning the tides and the role of photos in determining water depth during Tarawa planning sessions.

513. Emmons, Roger M. "Tarawa Bombardment." *Marine Corps Gazette*, XXXII (Mar. 1948), pp. 42-47. DN
Review of bombardment and Japanese preparations.

514. "The Fight for Tarawa." *Life*, XV (Dec. 13, 1944), pp. 27-35. DLC
Photographic account of battle.

515. Graham, Garrett. "Tarawa." *Marine Corps Gazette*, XXVIII (Apr. 1944), pp. 29-33. DN
Review of Robert Sherrod and his book.

516. Gregg, Charles T. *Tarawa*. New York: Stein & Day Pubs., 1984. 198 pp. DLC
Detailed history putting the battle into perspective.

517. Haley, J. Frederick. "Reconnaissance at Tarawa Atoll." *Marine Corps Gazette*, LXIV (Nov. 1980), pp. 51-55. DN
Review of the search for individuals familiar with and information concerning the beaches and tides at Betio.

518. Hammel, Eric M., and John E. Lane. "Third Day on Red Beach." *Marine Corps Gazette*, LIV (Nov. 1970), pp. 22-26. DN
Review of operations on Betio beach November 22, 1943.

519. _____. *76 Hours, The Invasion of Tarawa*. Pacifica, CA: Pacifica Press, 1985. 266 pp. DLC
Detailed account of the Battle for Betio.

520. Hannah, Dick. *Tarawa, the Toughest Battle in Marine Corps History*. New York: Duell, Sloan and Pearce, 1944. 126 pp. PCarlMH
Pictorial history.

521. Hoyt, Edwin P. *Storm Over the Gilberts, War in the Central Pacific, 1943*. New York: Mason/Charter, 1978. 162 pp. DLC
Popular account of the invasion.

522. Jonas, Carl. "My First Day on Tarawa." Saturday Evening Post, CCXVI (Mar. 4, 1944), pp. 22-23+. DLC
Author's experiences with invasion forces.

523. Jones, Edgar L. "Marooned on the Rock: What Has Happened to the Mechanics, SeeBees, and Ground Forces Left Behind." Atlantic Monthly, CLXXV (Apr. 1945), pp. 48-54. DLC
Commentary on the occupation forces on Tarawa.

524. Jones, William K. "Tarawa That Stinking Little Island." Marine Corps Gazette, LXXI (Nov. 1987), pp. 30-41. DN
Account of 6th Marines mopping up operations.

525. Kirkpatrick, Ralph Z. "The Tarawa and Makin Area a Century Ago." United States Naval Institute Proceedings, LXXII (Aug. 1946), pp. 1072. DN
Navy expedition of 1838-1842, comments concerning and description of the Gilbert Islands.

526. Ladd, Dean. "Reliving the Battle: A Return to Tarawa." Marine Corps Gazette, LXVII (Nov. 1983), pp. 93-98. DN
Recollections of a veteran based on a visit back to the island in 1983.

527. Mason, John T., Jr. editor. The Pacific War Remembered. An Oral History Collection. Annapolis, MD: Naval Institute Press, 1986. 373 pp. DN
Article by Carl E. Moore, "Assault on Tarawa and Apamama," pp. 172-177.

528. McKiernan, Patrick L. "Tarawa: The Tide that Failed." United States Naval Institute Proceedings, LXXXVIII (Feb. 1962), pp. 38-49. DN
Review of the information available at the time and the gamble that failed.

529. "The Men of Tarawa." New York Times Magazine, (Dec. 12, 1943), pp. 18-19. DLC
Brief commentary on grim toll of Tarawa.

530. Metcalf, Clyde H. "This Was Tarawa." Marine Corps Gazette, XXVIII (May 1944), pp. 45-48. DN
Review of battle, includes a copy of Presidential Unit Citation for the 2nd Marine Division.

531. Moore, W. Robert. "Gilbert Islands in the Wake of War." National Geographic, LXXXVII (Feb. 1945), pp. 129-162. DLC
Detailed account of post-combat activities.

532. Morrison, Samuel E. "Gilberts and Marshalls; Past of Recently Captured Pacific Groups." Life, XVI (May 22, 1944), pp. 90-100. DLC
Detailed account of operations with maps and drawings.

533. _____ History of United States Naval Operations in World War II; Vol. VII, Aleutians, Gilberts and Marshalls, June 1942-April 1944. Boston: Little, Brown and Co., 1951. 369 pp. DN
Navy's semi-official history of the War; it provides a comprehensive review of the campaigns in the Central Pacific.

534. Nalty, Bernard C. The United States Marines in the Gilbert Campaign. Washington: Historical Section, HQ, U.S. Marine Corps, 1961. (Revised 1962). 9 pp. DN
General account of the campaign.

535. "Operation Galvanic." After the Battle, 15 (1977), pp. 1-33.
Detailed review of the battle with then and now photographs.

536. "PFC Gross: Tarawa's Hub of Communications." Leatherneck, XXVIII (May 1944), pp. 53. DN
Account of radio man on Tarawa for 36 hours.

537. Pratt, Fletcher. "Tarawa: The Tough Nut." Marine Corps Gazette, XXXI (Apr. 1947), pp. 20-30. (Marines in the Pacific War, Part 8) DN
Comprehensive review of the battle.

538. Pratt, William V. "Lessons of the Tarawa Fighting." Newsweek, XXII (Dec. 13, 1943), pp. 37. DLC
Mentions shore bombardment.

539. _____ "The Significance of Our Seizure of the Gilberts." Newsweek, XXII (Dec. 6, 1943), pp. 24. DLC
Emphasizes air base potential.

540. "Report from Tarawa, Marines Story." Time, XLII (Dec. 6, 1943), pp. 24-35. DLC
First account of battle lacking detail.

541. Richardson, William. The Epic of Tarawa. London: Odhams Press, 1945. 96 pp.
Pictorial history for general reader.

542. Rixey, P. M. "Artillery at Tarawa." Marine Corps Gazette, XXVIII (Nov. 1944), pp. 32-37. DN
Account of artillery effectiveness.

543. Russ, Martin. Line of Departure: Tarawa. Garden City, NY: Doubleday & Co., 1975. 195 pp. PCarlMH
General account of the battle based in part on veteran reminiscences.

544. "Scene of Epic Struggle of the U.S. Marines with the Japanese." Illustrated London News, CCIII (Dec. 11, 1943), pp. 658-659.

545. "Sgt. Johnson: He Stopped a Tank with a Daring Act." Leatherneck, XXVII (Nov. 1944). DN
Story of Sgt. Roy W. Johnson, USMC winning the Navy Cross.

546. Shaw, Henry I. Tarawa: A Legend is Born. New York: Ballantine Books, 1968. 157 pp. DN
Hour by hour pictorial history.

547. Sherrod, Robert. "A Guy Named Hawkins." Marine Corps Gazette, LIV (Nov. 1970), pp. 27-29. DN
Account of Lt. Dean Hawkins, USMC who was killed on Tarawa.

548. _____. "Report on Tarawa." Time, XVII (Dec. 6, 1943), pp. 24-25. DLC
One of the first accounts of the battle.

549. _____. "Tarawa: The Second Day." Marine Corps Gazette, LVII (Nov. 1973), pp. 38-47. DN
Excerpts from title no. 553.

550. _____. Tarawa: The Story of a Battle. New York: Duell, Sloan and Pearce, 1944. 183 pp. DLC
One of the first and still considered one of the better accounts of the battle. Author was a war correspondent with Marines at Tarawa. Complete list of casualties.

551. _____. Tarawa: The Story of a Battle. Fredericksburg, TX: Admiral Nimitz Foundation, 1973. 206 pp. DN
Revised edition with author's reflections on the battle forty years later.

552. Simmons, Edward. "Tarawa Postscript." Fortitudine, XIII (Fall 1983), pp. 3-6. DN
Collection of letters and commentary on the Fortieth Anniversary of the battle.

553. Smith, Julian C. "Tarawa." United States Naval Institute Proceedings, LXXIX (Nov. 1953), pp. 1163-1175. DN
General Smith was commanding officer of 2nd Marine Division; provides insight to operations and command decisions.

554. Stern, Michael. Into the Jaws of Death. New York: Robert M. McBride & Co., 1944. 237 pp. DLC
Includes a firsthand account concerning Tarawa.

555. Stockman, James R. The Battle for Tarawa. Washington: Historical Section, Division of Public Information, HQ, U.S. Marine Corps, 1947. 86 pp. DLC (reprinted by Battery Press, 1986)
Comprehensive account of the operation with very heavy emphasis on Marine participation.

556. "Tarawa: Marines Win New Glory in the Gilberts and Prove There Is No Cheap Victory." Life, XV (Dec. 6, 1943), p. 36. DLC
Photographic review.

557. "This was Tarawa." Time, LXII (Dec. 13, 1943), pp. 24-25. DLC
Photographic review.

558. Tolbert, Frank X. "Apamama - A Model Operation in Miniature." Leatherneck, XXVIII (Feb. 1945), pp. 26-27. DN
Account of Reconnaissance Marines capturing Apamama.

559. _____. "Death at Close Quarters." Leatherneck, XXVII (July 1944), pp. 38-39. DN
Account of fighting on Betio.

560. _____. "Mop-up Beyond Betio." Leatherneck, XXVII (June 1944), p. 36. DN
Account of Cpl. Arlton K. Wallace, USMC, mopping-up stray Japanese.

561. _____. "Tarawa, A Year Later." Leatherneck, XXVII (Nov. 1944), pp. 26-29. DN
Review of situation.

562. _____. "Winning Pitcher: Spillane." Leatherneck, XXVII (Aug. 1944), pp. 28-29. DN
Story of Sgt. John J. Spillane, USMC winning the Navy Cross.

563. U.S. Army. Central Pacific Base Command. G-4. Final Close Out Report on Gilbert. 1 July 1945. n.p.: HQ, Central Pacific Base Command, 1945. 25 pp. PCarlMH

564. U.S. Army Forces in the Pacific. G-4. Galvanic Operation. 14 June 1944. n.p.: HQ, U.S. Army Forces in the Pacific, D-4, 1944. 200 pp. PCarlMH
Operations plan for Gilbert Island operations.

565. U.S. Joint Intelligence Center. Enemy Positions: The Gilbert Islands, Ocean and NAVRA. n.p.: U.S. Joint Intelligence Center, Pacific Ocean Areas, 1943. 2 vols. Mimeo PCarlMH

566. _____ Enemy Positions: The Marshall-Gilbert Area. n.p.: U.S. Joint Intelligence Center, Pacific Ocean Areas, 1943. 118 pp. Mimeo PCarlMH

567. _____ Gilbert Islands: Objective Folder. n.p.: U.S. Joint Intelligence Center, Pacific Ocean Areas, 1943. 25 pp. Mimeo PCarlMH

568. _____ Information of Enemy Positions, Central Pacific Area. n.p.: U.S. Joint Intelligence Center, Pacific Ocean Areas, 1942. 37 pp. Mimeo PCarlMH

569. _____ Study of Japanese Defenses of Betio Island (Tarawa Atoll). San Francisco: c/o Fleet Post Office, 1944. 52 pp. PCarlMH

570. U.S. Navy, Office of the Chief of Naval Operations, Intelligence Division. "Combat Narratives." unpublished paper: Chief Naval Operations, Office of Naval Intelligence, 1942-1945. DN
    The Capture of the Gilberts. 75 pp.
Combat Narrative taken from what was originally classified or non-published documents. See also under Marshall Islands, No. 601.

GILBERT ISLANDS OPERATIONS 69

571. Werstein, Irving. *Tarawa: A Battle Report*. New York: Crowell, 1965. 146 pp. DN
Popular history for juvenile readers.

572. Wertenbaker, Green P. "Appointment in Tarawa." *New Yorker*, XIX (Feb. 12, 1944), pp. 52+. DLC
Observations of life aboard a carrier before a strike in the Gilberts.

573. "Where the U.S. Marines Won a Great Victory." *London Illustrated News*, CCIII (Dec. 18, 1943), p. 676.

574. Willard, W. Weyth. *The Leathernecks Come Through*. New York: Fleming H. Revell Co., 1944. 224 pp. DLC
Chaplain's account of service in the Solomons and Gilberts operations.

575. Wilson, Earl J., and others. *Betio Beachhead: U.S. Marines' Own Story of the Battle for Tarawa: An Account Documented and Written by Four Marines Who Went Through the Battle*. New York: Putnam, 1945. 160 pp. DLC
Composite history of the battle by USMC combat correspondents.

576. Wukovits, John F. "Even Hell Wouldn't Have It." *American History Illustrated*, XX (Feb. 1986), pp. 38-48. DLC
General review of the battle.

6.
Marshall Islands Operations

GENERAL WORKS

577. "Action in the Marshalls." Time, XXXIX (Feb. 23, 1942), pp. 21-22. DLC
Brief account of early raid.

578. "Battle in the Pacific." Time, XLIII (Feb. 7, 1944), pp. 18-19. DLC
Brief review of Marshall Islands campaign.

579. DeChant, John A. "Marine Aviation in the Battle for the Marshalls." Marine Corps Gazette, XXXI (June 1947), pp. 27-34. (Marines in the Pacific, Part 5) DN
General account of Marine Aviation in the battle.

580. Durant, John. "We Sank an Island." Colliers, CXIV (July 1, 1944), p. 69. DLC
Brief review of the capture of an island adjacent to Kwajalein for artillery placement.

581. Heinl, Robert D., Jr., and John A. Crown. The Marshalls: Increasing the Tempo. Washington: Historical Branch, G-3 Division Headquarters, U.S. Marine Corps, 1954. 180 pp. (Marine Monograph Series) ND
Excellent account of the operations with emphasis on Marine participation.

582. Hill, Harry W. "The Marshall Islands Operation." Military Review, XXVIII (Jan. 1948), pp. 3-11; (Feb. 1948), pp. 51-54. PCarlMH
Detailed account of operations.

583. "Marshall Islands Invaded." United States Naval Institute Proceedings, LXX (Mar. 1944), pp. 346-347. DN
Brief review compiled from newspaper releases.

584. Marshalls - Gilberts Area, Military Government Section. "A Report on the U.S. Navy Military Government of the Marshall Islands for the Year 31 January 1944 to 21 January 1945." unpublished paper: Naval Forces, 1945. 38 pp. ND
Report covering the Naval Administration of the Marshall Islands, the first Japanese mandated islands placed under U.S. military occupation.

585. Metcalf, Clyde H. "In the Big League Phase." Marine Corps Gazette, XXVIII (Apr. 1944), pp. 17-20. DN
Review of Pacific campaigns to 1944.

586. Moore, W. Robert. "Marshallese are Happy Again." National Geographic, LXXXVIII (Sept. 1945), pp. 337-360. DLC
Pictorial review of islander activities.

587. _____ "Our new Military Wards, the Marshalls." National Geographic, LXXXVIII (Sept. 1945), pp. 325-336. DLC
Review of American occupation and bases.

588. Moorehouse, Clifford P. "Securing the Marshalls." Marine Corps Gazette, XXVIII (Apr. 1944), pp. 21+. DN
Brief review of battle.

589. Nalty, Bernard C. The United States Marines in the Marshall Campaign. Washington: Historical Branch, USMC, 1962. 9 pp. Marine Corps Reference Series, No. 31. DN
Detailed account of the campaign.

590. "Pacific War: The U.S. Conquest of the Marshall Islands and the Successful Raid on Truk." Illustrated London News, CCIV (Apr. 1, 1944), pp. 380-381.

591. Pratt, Fletcher. "The Marshalls: Offensive in High Gear." Marine Corps Gazette, XXX (May 1947), pp. 32-42. (Marines in the Pacific War, Part 9) DN
Detailed account of the capture.

592. "Researched at Tarawa." Time, XLIII (Feb. 14, 1944), pp. 26-28. DLC
Review of Marshall Island operations.

593. "Softening the Marshalls: 160 Sq. Miles of Sand, Coral, and Coconut Palms." Time, XLII (Dec. 27, 1943), pp. 25-27. DLC
Brief review of air operations against various atolls in the Marshalls.

594. Trefethan, E. M. "Air Battle for the Marshalls." Leatherneck, XXVII (Sept. 1944), pp. 38-39. DN
General account of the Fourth Marine Air Wing in the battle.

MARSHALL ISLANDS OPERATIONS 73

595. U.S. Army, Central Pacific Area. Marshall Islands, Japanese Defenses and Battle Damage. n.p.: HQ, Central Pacific Area, 1944. 58 pp. ND
Report of the defenses used by the Japanese in the Marshalls with some references to Tarawa. Based on interviews, direct observation and photographs.

596. U.S. Army, Central Pacific Base Command. G-4. Marshall-Gilbert Army Area. n.p.: 1945. 42 pp. PCarlMH
History of four major islands: Makin Atoll, Apamama Atoll, Kwajalein Island (Atoll), and Engeli Island (Atoll).

597. U.S. Joint Intelligence Center, Pacific Ocean Areas. Study of Japanese Installations on Butaritari Island and Makin Atoll. San Francisco: c/o Fleet Post Office, 1944. 160 pp. PCarlMH

598. U.S. Navy, United States Pacific Fleet, Commander-in-Chief. Battle Experiences. Vol. 17. "Battle Experiences, Supporting Operations for the Occupation of the Marshall Islands, including Eniwetok. February 1944." unpublished paper: Chief of Naval Operations, 1943-1945. DN
Account of the lessons learned during the operations.

599. _____ Amphibious Operations in the Marshall Islands, January-February 1944. n.p.: U.S. Fleet, CominCh, 1944.

600. U.S. Navy, Commander in Chief, U.S. Pacific Fleet. "Administrative History of the ComMarGils Area." unpublished papers: 1946. 6 vols. DN
Comprehensive wartime administrative history of the naval forces in the Gilberts and Marshall Islands areas; includes a chronology.

601. U.S. Navy, Intelligence Division, Office of the Chief of Naval Operations. "Combat Narratives." unpublished papers: Chief Naval Operations, Office of Naval Intelligence, 1942-1945. DN
   The Assault on Kwajalein and Majuro. (Part 1) 92 pp.
   Early Raids in the Pacific, 1 February - 10 March 1942. 71 pp.
Combat narratives taken from what were originally classified or non-published documents.

602. U.S. Strategic Bombing Survey. The American Campaign Against Wotje, Maloelap, Mille and Jaluit. Washington: Government Printing Office, 1947. 375 pp. DLC
Detailed account of the air campaign.

603. "Victory in the Marshalls." Infantry Journal, LIV (Apr. 1944), pp. 26-29. PCarlMH
Pictorial review.

ENIWETOK ATOLL

604. Carleton, Phillip D. "The Taking of Eniwetok." *Marine Corps Gazette*, XXVIII (May 1944), pp. 19-23. DN
General account of the battle.

605. Kelly, Lt. R. J., USMC, and others. "Command History, Eniwetok Atoll." unpublished paper: Admin. Hist. Appen. 38 (31), 1945. 320 pp. DN
History of the command from the island's occupation to the establishment of Naval Operating Base Enewetok in June 1945.

606. "Marines Take Eniwetok." *Marine Corps Gazette*, XXVIII (Apr. 1944), pp. 22-23. DN
Brief pictorial review.

607. Meyer, Cord. "On the Beaches." *Atlantic Monthly*, CLXXIV (Oct. 1944), pp. 42. DLC
Author's experiences on Eniwetok.

608. Wilcox, Richard. "The Battle of Eniwetok Atoll." *Life*, XVI (Mar. 13, 1944), pp. 21-25. DLC
Detailed account of landing on Engebi.

609. _____ "Marines Take Eniwetok." *Marine Corps Gazette*, XXVIII (Aug. 1944), pp. 28. DN
Photographic review.

KWAJALEIN ATOLL

610. Arnold, MG Archibald V. Kwajalein Atoll - An Interim Report. *Field Artillery*, XXXIV (Sept. 1944), pp. 595-596. PCarlMH
Comments on artillery operations.

611. "The Battle of Kwajalein." *Newsweek*, XLIII (Feb. 14, 1944), pp. 22-26. DLC
Review of Marshall's invasion and Allied leadership in Central Pacific.

612. The Battle of Kwajalein and Roi-Namur. n.p.: 1981. 64 pp.
Detailed study including maps.

613. English, Richard. "Seagoing Taxi No. 1: The Coast Guard's Ace Transport from Casablanca to Kwajalein." *Saturday Evening Post*, CCXVI (June 24, 1944), pp. 22-23. DLC

614. Hunt, Frazier. "Kwajalein Becomes a Mighty Base." *Saturday Evening Post*, CCXVI (Mar. 25, 1944), pp. 22+. DLC
Review of destruction of reconstruction of Kwajalein Island.

615. "Kwajalein." Marine Corps Gazette, XXVIII (Mar. 1944), pp. 32-33. DN
Very brief pictorial review.

616. "Kwajalein Glimpse." Field Artillery, XXXIV (July 1944), p. 457. PCarlMH
Extracts from a field artillery officer's letter concerning Kwajalein.

617. "The Lesson of Kwajalein." Newsweek, XXIII (Feb. 21, 1944), pp. 26-28. DLC
Comments on Allied and Japanese reaction to the Marshalls' capture.

618. Marshall, Samuel L. A. "The After-Action Interview--the Kwajalein Experience." Army, XVI (Sept. 1966), pp. 58-61. PCarlMH

619. U.S. Navy, Kwajalein Naval Base. "Command History of the U.S. Naval Base Kwajalein." unpublished paper: Admin. Hist. Appen. 38 (16) (C), 1945. 220 pp. DN
Comprehensive account of the Kwajalein Naval Base from its inception in late 1943 to July 1945.

620. Wilcox, Richard. "Kwajalein." Life, XVI (Feb. 21, 1944), pp. 34-37. DLC
Photographic review of the island's destruction.

MAJURO

621. "The Little Ones Count, Too." Leatherneck, XXVII (Sept. 1944), pp. 32-34. DN
Account of the taking of the small islands in the Marshalls.

MAKIN

622. Aquilina, Robert V. "Who Was Left Behind on Makin?" Fortitudine, XIX (Summer 1989), pp. 22-23. DN
Account of the nine marines captured on Makin during the first raid.

623. Karig, Walter. "The Makin Island Raid." United States Naval Institute Proceedings, LXX (Oct. 1946), pp. 1277-1282. DN
Brief account of 1942 raid.

624. LeFrancois, Wilfred S. "We Mopped Up Makin Island." Saturday Evening Post, CCXVI (Dec. 4, 1943), pp. 20-21+; (Dec. 11, 1943), pp. 28-29+. DLC
Account concerning Carlson's raiders.

625. "Makin Atoll." Infantry Journal, LIV (Feb. 1944), pp. 19-20. PCarlMH
Pictorial review.

626. Marlowe, W. H. "Taking Makin." Infantry Journal, LIV (June 1944), pp. 28-30. PCarlMH
Firsthand accounts.

627. Marshall, Samuel L. A. "Fight on Saki Night: An Episode in the Conquest of Makin." Infantry Journal, LIV (Apr. 1944), pp. 8-15. PCarlMH
Detailed account of 27th Infantry Division operations on Makin.

628. Peatross, Oscar T. "The Makin Raid." Marine Corps Gazette, LXIII (Nov. 1979), pp. 96-103 pp. DN
Review of the first Makin Island raid in August 1942.

629. U.S. Army, Central Pacific Base Command. G-4. Final Close Out Report on Makin. 1 July 1945. n.p.: HQ, Central Pacific Base Command, 1945. 30 pp. PCarlMH

See also 77th Infantry Division, title nos. 831-834.

ROI-NAMUR

630. Bishop, John. "The Battle of the Drains: Roi and Namur Islands." Saturday Evening Post, CCXVI (June 3, 1944), pp. 20-22+. DLC
General account by eyewitness of the assault phase of the operation.

631. "Four Coast Guardmen Capture Nine Japs." U.S. Coast Guard Academy Alumni Association Bulletin, VI (Apr. 1944), pp. 17. DLC
Actions during the invasion of Roi-Namur.

632. Heinl, Robert D. "D-Day, Roi-Namur." Military Affairs, XII (1948), pp. 129-141. PCarlMH
Detailed account of the capture of Roi-Namur.

633. Leary, R. T. "Semper Paratus." United States Naval Institute Proceedings, LXXVIII (Apr. 1944), pp. 405-413. DN
Author commanded a Coast Guard manned LST during Roi and Namur operations.

634. Macmillan, I. E. "Naval Gunfire at Roi-Namur." Marine Corps Gazette, XXXII (July 1948), pp. 50-55. DN
Review of effectiveness of naval gunfire support.

635. Tolbert, Frank X. "The Ear-banger on Namur." Leatherneck, XXVII (May 1944), p. 21. DN
Account of torpedo stockpile exploding.

636. Wharton, Don. "He Led the Fight on Kwajalein. Now Capt. Jimmy Denig of the Marines in the First Conquered Enemy Soil..." Look, VIII (Sept. 19, 1944), pp. 38-39. DLC
Brief account of tank action led by Capt. James L. Denig on Namur Island.

7.
Marianas Islands Operations

GENERAL WORKS

637. <u>Campaign for the Marianas</u>. Washington: Historical Division, HQ, U.S.M.C., 1946. 91 pp. DN
Brief account of operations.

638. Caporale, Louis G. "Prelude to Victory: The Marianas." <u>Marine Corps Gazette</u>, LXVIII (June 1984), pp. 18-27. DN
Review of the amphibious operations.

639. Crowl, Philip A. <u>Campaign in the Marianas</u>. Washington: Office of the Chief of Military History [Government Printing Office], 1960. PCarlMH (U.S. Army in World War II series)
Official history of the Army's participation in the campaign, providing a comprehensive overview of the strategic and tactical operations.

640. "Deadlier than Volcanoes: The Battle for Saipan Island." <u>Newsweek</u>, XXIV (July 10, 1944), pp. 33. DLC
Brief account of war in the Central Pacific and casualties.

641. Draper, William F. "Victory's Portrait in the Marianas." <u>National Geographic</u>, LXXXVIII (Nov. 1945), pp. 599-616. DLC
General pictorial account.

642. Hoyt, Edwin P. <u>To the Marianas: War in the Central Pacific, 1944</u>. New York: Van Nostrand Reinhold, 1980. 292 pp. DLC
Popular history with emphasis on individual accounts.

643. Price, Willard. "Springboard to Tokyo." <u>National Geographic</u>, LXXXVI (Oct. 1944), pp. 385-407. DLC
Detailed review of the importance of the Marianas.

78   THE CENTRAL PACIFIC CAMPAIGN, 1943-1944

644. Sherrod, Robert L. "Beachhead in the Marianas." Time, XLIV (July 3, 1944), pp. 32-33. DLC
Firsthand account of action on Saipan.

645. _____. On to Westward! War in the Central Pacific. New York: Duell, Sloan and Pearce, 1945. 333 pp. DLC
Popular account of Central Pacific invasions, particularly the Marianas.

646. "To the Victor: The Bases." Time, XLIV (July 17, 1944), pp. 28-29. DLC
Brief account of campaign.

647. U.S. Armed Forces in the Central Pacific Area. Participation in the Marianas Operation. n.p.: U.S. Army Forces in the Central Pacific, 1944. 2 vols. PCarlMH

648. U.S. Navy, Office of the Chief of Naval Operations, Division of Naval Intelligence. "ONI 29, Palau and Marianas Islands." Washington: 1942.

649. Zimmerman, Sherwood R. "Operation Forager." United States Naval Institute Proceedings, XC (Aug. 1964), pp. 78-90. DN
Review of the operations to take the Marianas.

AIR OPERATIONS

650. Bensen, Douglass L. "A Few Enchanted Evenings." Aerospace Historian, XXIX (Fall 1982), pp. 186-190. DN
Author's experiences with air service group at Isely Field on Saipan.

651. Crossley, R. P. "Damn the Submarines! Turn on the Lights." Popular Mechanics, CXXXI (June 1969), pp. 111-115. DLC
Decision to light the carriers for returning airmen.

652. Denfield, D. Colt. "Isely Field. World War II in the Pacific." America's Military Past, IV (Dec. 1983), pp. 3-12.
Includes Japanese Air Depot and U.S. Base operations.

653. Flick, Alvin S. "The Great Marianas Turkey Shoot." Aviation Quarterly, V (Fall 1979), pp. 214-235.
Comprehensive review of the air operations.

654. Land, William G., and Adrian O. Van Wyen. "Naval Air Operations in the Marianas." unpublished paper   Individual Personnel, 1945. 165 pp. DN
Comprehensive analysis of the operations drawn from official publications, dispatches, and reports. Provides statistical data for the preparations as well as the operations themselves.

655. Miller, Thomas G., Jr. "Anatomy of an Air Battle." American Aviation Historical Society Journal, XV (Summer 1970), pp. 115-120.
Review of the air operations in the Battle for the Marianas.

656. Rust, Kenneth C. "They Fell Like Flies." RAF Flying Review, XVI (July 1961), pp. 30-32.
Brief account of air battle.

NAVAL OPERATIONS

657. "The Big Blow - Philippine Sea, 1944." All Hands, No. 542, (Mar. 1962), pp. 59-63. DN

658. Buell, Thomas B. "The Battle for the Philippine Sea." United States Naval Institute Proceedings, C (July 1974), pp. 64-84.
Comprehensive review of issues facing commanders.

659. Clark, Joseph J. "The Marianas Turkey Shoot." American Heritage, XVIII (Oct. 1967), pp. 26-29+. DLC
Excerpts from author's memoirs, see number 435.

660. Danton, J. Periam. "The Battle for the Philippine Sea." United States Naval Institute Proceedings, LXXI (Sept. 1945), pp. 1023-1027. DN
Author's recollections of battle.

661. Dickson, W. D. The Battle of the Philippine Sea. London: Allan, 1975. 100 pp. (Sea Battles in Close-up)
Brief history for the general reader.

662. Lockwood, Charles A. Battles of the Philippine Sea. New York: Y. Crowell Co., 1967. 229 pp. DLC
Popular history of the battle.

663. Morrison, Samuel E. History of United States Naval Operations in World War II. Vol. VIII. New Guinea and the Marianas, March 1944 - Aug 1944. Boston: Little, Brown & Co., 1953. 435 pp. DN
Volume from the Navy's Official History of Naval Operation during the War. A comprehensive and readable account.

664. Smith, Allan E. "Battle of the Philippine Sea." United States Naval Institute Proceedings, C (Nov. 1974), pp. 102. DN
Comments on Admiral Spruance.

665. U.S. Navy, United States Pacific Fleet, Commander-in-Chief. Battle Experiences. Vol. 20. "Battle Experiences, Supporting Operations for the capture of the Marianas Islands (Saipan, Guam, and Tinian), June - August 1944." unpublished paper: Chief of Naval Operations, 1943-1945. DN
Account of the lessons learned during the operations.

666. Van Wyen, Adrian O. "The Battle of the Philippine Sea." United States Naval Institute Proceedings, LXXVII (Feb. 1951), pp. 156-159. DN
Detailed account.

80 THE CENTRAL PACIFIC CAMPAIGN, 1943-1944

667. Winston, Robert A. "How Our Navy Outfoxed the Japs at Saipan." Saturday Evening Post, CCXVII (Sept. 23, 1944), pp. 19+. DLC
Account of air operations during the Battle of the Philippine Sea.

668. "Worth the Price: Strategic Saipan Tough Nut for U.S. Navy Pushing East." Newsweek, XXIII (June 26, 1944), p. 38. DLC
Brief review of battle with maps.

669. Y'Blood, William T. Red Sun Setting: The Battle of the Philippine Sea. Annapolis: Naval Institute Press, 1981. 257 pp. DN
Detailed history with emphasis on participant viewpoints.

SAIPAN

670. Appleman, Roy E. Army Tanks in the Battle for Saipan. n.p.: 1945. 223 pp. Typescript   PCarlMH

671. "Bloody Saipan." Newsweek, XXIV (July 24, 1944), p. 37. DLC
Brief commentary on U.S. and Japanese casualties.

672. "Deadlier than Volcanoes: The Battle for Saipan Island." Newsweek, XXIV (July 10, 1944), p. 38. DLC
Very brief account of operations, casualties, and Japanese and American press releases.

673. Donovan, James A. "Saipan Tank Battle." Marine Corps Gazette, XXXII (Oct. 1948), pp. 25-31. DN
Provides a descriptive review of a Japanese tank attack.

674. Doying, George. "The Buck Rogers Men." Leatherneck, XXVIII (Apr. 1945), pp. 27-29. DN
Review of the use of the bazooka by Marines on Saipan and Tinian.

675. _____ "Thirty Days on the Line." Leatherneck, XXVII (Dec. 1944), pp. 18-20. DN
Detailed account of a 4th Marine Division company on Saipan.

676. _____ "War on Japan's Doorstep, the Battle for Saipan." Leatherneck, XXVII (Sept. 1944), pp. 15-19. DN
Story of Col. Chambers' raiders on Saipan.

677. "Generals Smith." Time, XLIV (Sept. 18, 1944), pp. 66, 68. DLC
Brief comments regarding his relief of MG Ralph Smith.

678. Goe, William. Is War Hell? Los Angeles: Privately printed, 1947. 270 pp.
Memoirs of a Marine chaplain who served on Saipan.

679. Grahane, A. "Recording the Saipan Fight on Wire." Popular Science, CVL (Dec. 1944), p. 201. DLC
Brief account of tape recording interviews and battle sounds.

MARIANAS ISLANDS OPERATIONS

680. Haffert, William A. "This Was Saipan." U.S. Coast Magazine, XVIII (Dec. 1944), p. 38.

681. Hilton, Robert M. "We Landed at Saipan." U.S. Coast Guard Academy Association Bulletin, VI (Oct. 1944), p. 143. DLC

682. Hockmuth, Bruno A. "Observations on Saipan." Marine Corps Gazette, XXIX (Jan. 1945), pp. 36-38. DN
Account of June 15-19 operations on Saipan.

683. HQ, Northern Troops and Landing Force. Marianas Phase I (Saipan). August 1944. n.p.: HQ, Northern Troops and Landing Force, 1944. PCarlMH

684. Hoffman, Carl W. Saipan: The Beginning of the End. Washington: Historical Division, HQ, U.S. Marine Corps, 1950. 286 pp. (Marine Monographs) DN
Comprehensive account of the operation with heavy emphasis on the Marine Corps participation.

685. Jones, Don. OBA, the Last Samurai: Saipan, 1944-1945. Novato, CA: Presidio Press, 1986. 241 pp. DLC
Popular account of a Japanese soldier who served on island.

686. Kinkead, E. "Fires on Saipan." New Yorker, XX (Sept 2, 1944), pp. 42-49. DLC
Eyewitness account of pre-invasion bombardment aboard a battleship.

687. Love, Edmund G. "Army Says Holland Smith Is Wrong." Saturday Evening Post, CCXXI (Nov. 13, 1948), pp. 33+. DLC
Army's version of MG Smith's relief on Saipan.

688. _____. "Smith vs. Smith." Infantry Journal, VXIII (Nov. 1948), pp. 3-13. PCarlMH
Review of battle and the relief of Army MG Ralph Smith.

689. "Mopping Up Saipan." Life, 17 (July 24, 1944), pp. 26-29. DLC
Photographic review of clearing Japanese holdouts.

690. Saipan. Washington(?): ca1944. 18 pp. ViU

691. Morris, Frank D. "The Battle at Saipan." Collier's, CXIV (Aug. 13, 1944), pp. 16+. DLC
General account of battle.

692. Morton, Louis. "The Marianas." Military Review, XLVII (July 1967), pp. 71-82. PCarlMH
Brief review of campaign.

693. Sherrod, Robert. "An Answer & Rebuttal to "Smith vs. Smith: the Saipan Controversy." Infantry Journal, LXIV (Jan. 1949), pp. 14-28. PCarlMH
Marine correspondent's account of actions leading to MG Smith's relief.

694. _____ "Beachhead in the Marianas." Time, XLIV (July 3, 1944), pp. 32-34. DLC
Firsthand account of operations on Saipan.

695. _____ "Gone to Earth." Time, XLIV (July 17, 1944), p. 28. DLC
Account concerning the clearing of snipers.

696. _____ "Last Charge." Time, XLIV (July 24, 1944), pp. 26-28. DLC
Review of Saipan operations.

697. _____ "Saipan: Eyewitness Tells of Island Fight." Life, XVII (Aug. 28, 1944), pp. 75-83. DLC
Photographic account of Saipan battles.

698. _____ "Battalion on Saipan," Marine Corps Gazette, XXVIII (Oct. 1944), pp. 10-16. DN
Review of 1st Bn, 6th Marines operations.

699. Schubert, Paul. "Saipan and Pacific Strategy." Marine Corps Gazette, XXVIII (Aug. 1944), pp. 33-35. DN
Review of American capture of island.

700. Smith, Holland M. "My Troubles with the Army on Saipan." Saturday Evening Post, CCXXI (Nov. 13, 1948), pp. 32+. DLC
Account of his relations with the Army and the 27th Infantry Division.

701. Stockman, James R. "The Taking of Mount Topatchou." Marine Corps Gazette, XXXII (Oct. 1948), pp. 15+. DN
Provides a comprehensive account of actions taken in seizing the mountain.

702. Turner, Gordon B. The Amphibious Complex: a Study of Operations at Guam. PhD Thesis, Princeton University, 1950. NjP

703. U.S. Department of Army. Foreign Mine Warfare Equipment. TM 5-280. April 1963. n.p.: Government Printing Office, 1963. 984 pp.
Reviews the Japanese usage of mines on Saipan including descriptions and maps of mine fields. Also describes the various types of mines used by the Japanese during WWII.

704. U.S. Navy, Intelligence Division, Office of the Chief of Naval Operations. Combat Narratives. n.p.: Chief Naval Operations, Office of Naval Intelligence, 1942-1945. DN
    Operations in the Marianas Phase I: The Conquest of Saipan. 65 pp.
Combat Narrative taken from what were originally classified or non-published documents.

705. U.S. Navy, Pacific Fleet & Pacific Ocean Area. AA Defense of Saipan. Special Translation No. 36. n.p.: ca1944.
Report concerning the Japanese anti-aircraft defenses of Saipan.

706. Zurlinden, Cyril P. "Prelude to Saipan." United States Naval Institute Proceedings, LXXIII (May 1947), pp. 581-84. DN
Correspondent's recollection of pre-invasion bombardment and activities.

TINIAN

707. Army Times, editors of. The Tangled Web: True Stories of Deception in Modern Warfare. Washington: Robert B. Luce, 1963. DN
Contains account of the pre-invasion maneuvers at Tinian, pp. 148-157.

708. Hoffman, Carl W. The Seizure of Tinian. Washington: Historical Division, HQ, U.S. Marine Corps, 1951. 169 pp. DN (Marine Monographs)
One of the best accounts of the battle with emphasis on Marine participation.

709. Schmidt, R. K. "The Tinian Operation: A Study in Planning for Amphibious Operations." n.p.: unpublished paper, Senior Course, U.S.M.C. Amphibious Warfare School, Quantico, Va., 1949.
Review of the operational and logistical planning for the Tinian operation.

710. U.S. Navy, Pacific Fleet & Pacific Ocean Area. Tinian--Target Analysis Bulletin, Cincpac-Cincpoa Bulletin 67-44. n.p.: 1944.

GUAM

711. Beers, Henry P. American Naval Occupation and Government of Guam, 1898-1902. Washington: Department of Navy, 1944. 76 pp. DN
Description of the American capture of the island in June of 1898, as well as a description of its history and geography.

712. Conolly, Richard M., and others. "Combat Leadership." Marine Corps Gazette, XXXVI (Nov. 1946), pp. 24-31. DN
Reviews Sprunce's role in capture of Guam.

713. Cushman, Robert E. "The Fight at Fonte." Marine Corps Gazette, XXXVII (Apr. 1947), pp. 10-16. DN
Detailed account of action.

714. De Valle, BG Pedro A. "Guam, the Classical Amphibious Operation." Military Review, XXVII (Apr. 1947). pp. 4-12. PCarlMH
Author was Commanding Officer, III Amphibious Corps Artillery during the Guam invasion.

715. _____ "Massed Fire on the Island of Guam." Marine Corps Gazette, XXVIII (Dec. 1944), pp. 19-25. DN
Detailed account of artillery employment during the Battle for Guam.

716. _____ and John A. Bemis. "Sea Island Serenade: The Recapture of Guam." Field Artillery Journal, XXXIV (Dec. 1944), pp. 803-806. PCarlMH
General account of the recapture of Guam with emphasis on artillery.

717. Farrell, Don A. The Pictorial History of Guam: The Americanization: 1898-1918 and the Liberation: 1944. Tamuning, Guam: Micronesian Productions, 1984. 2 vols. DLC
Volume two covers the Japanese occupation and its liberation by American forces.

718. Francis, Anthony A. "The Battle for Banzai Ridge." Marine Corps Gazette, XXIX (June 1945), pp. 13-18. DN
Account of taking of cliff areas and Japanese counterattack.

719. Gailey, Harry A. The Liberation of Guam: 21 July-10 August 1944. Novato, CA: Presidio Press, 1988. 231 pp. DLC
Detailed account of battle.

720. Gore, W. B. "An Airfield Is Put in Operation." Marine Corps Gazette, XXIX (June 1945), pp. 36-39. DN
Pictorial account of the reconstruction of airfield at Orote.

721. "Guam and Tinian: The Pre-landing Bombardment." Newsweek, XXIV (July 31, 1944), pp. 40-45. DLC
Very brief account of operations and leaders.

722. Ito, Masashi. The Emperor's Last Soldiers. Translated by Roger Clifton. New York: Coward-McCann, Inc., 1967. 191 pp. PCarlMH
Account of a Japanese Army Sergeant who hid and survived on Guam from 1944 to 1960.

723. Johnson, Lucius W. "Guam - Before December 1941." United States Naval Institute Proceedings, LXVIII (July 1946), pp. 991-1006. DN
Useful for providing a pre-war picture of garrison life on the island.

724. Karig, Walter. "U.S. Navy Report on Guam, 1899-1950: History of Guam under Naval Administration." unpublished report: Individual Reports, 1950. 41 pp. DN

725. Kaufman, Millard. "The Attack on Guam." Marine Corps Gazette, XXIX (Apr. 1945), pp. 2-5+. DN
Generalized account of the battle focusing on the 1st Marine Provisional Brigade.

726. Klein, Edwin H. "The Handling of Supplies on Guam." Marine Corps Gazette, XXIX (Feb. 1945), pp. 25-27. DN
Review of shore party and field depot operations.

727. Larsen, Henry L. "Rehabilitation on Guam." Marine Corps Gazette, XXIX (June 1945), pp. 18-22. DN
Review of the reconstruction of the civilian sector.

MARIANAS ISLANDS OPERATIONS   85

728. *The Liberation of Guam.* n.p.: ca1979. [24] pp. DN
General account of the recapture of the island by army and marine troops.

729. Lodge, O. R. *The Recapture of Guam.* Washington: Historical Branch, HQ, U.S. Marine Corps, 1954. 214 pp. (Marine Monographs) DN
Best single volume history concerning the operation.

730. McMillan, I. E. "Naval Gunfire at Guam." *Marine Corps Gazette,* XXXII (Sept. 1948), pp. 52-56. DN
Detailed account of employment of naval gunfire.

731. _____. "One Step Short of Tokyo, Guam." *Popular Science,* LXXXIV (Nov. 1945), pp. 43-46+. DLC

732. Marek, Stephan. *Laughter in Hell...Being the True Experiences of Lieutenant E. L. Guirey, U.S.N. and Technical Sergeant H. C. Nixon, U.S.M.C. and Their Comrades in the Japanese Prison Camps in Osaka and Tsuruga.* Caldwell, ID: Caxton Printers, 1954. 256 pp. DN
Provides a review of the Japanese capture of Guam in 1941.

733. Nelson, F. J. "Guam. Our Western Outpost." *United States Naval Institute Proceedings,* LXVI (Jan. 1940), pp. 83-96. DN
Brief history of island.

734. Pickering, William T. "Mr. Dampier Also Went to Guam - in 1636." *United States Naval Institute Proceedings,* MXXI (Aug. 1945), pp. 931-935. DN
Comments on importance of Guam to Spain.

735. Pomeroy, Earl S. *Pacific Outpost: America's Strategy in Guam and Micronesia.* Stanford: Stanford Univ. Press, 1951. 198 pp. PCarlMH
Detailed review of Guam with emphasis on the diplomatic aspects.

736. Pratt, William V. "Prize of the Marianas: Guam Important to Our Strategy." *Newsweek,* XXIV (July 24, 1944), p. 26. DLC
Review of importance of Guam.

737. "Return to Guam." *Time,* XLIV (July 31, 1944), p. 25. DLC
Brief account of operations.

738. Rowcliff, Gilbert J. "Guam." *United States Naval Institute Proceeding,* LXXI (July 1945), pp. 781-793. DN
Account of U. S. recapture of the island.

739. Smith, Craig B. "A Guam Diary, Part 1, Japanese 'Straggler's' Notes Intrigue Researcher at Center." *Fortitudine,* XVII (Fall 1987), pp. 12-14. DN
Reviews a recently discovered diary by Sgt. Masashi Itoh, IJA, who surrendered in 1960.

740. Smith, H. E. "I Saw the Morning Break." *United States Naval Institute Proceedings,* LXXII (Mar. 1946), pp. 403-415. DN
Eyewitness account of the Guam Landing.

86 THE CENTRAL PACIFIC CAMPAIGN, 1943-1944

741. Thompson, Laura. <u>Guam and Its People</u>. Princeton, NJ: Princeton Univ. Press, 1947. 367 pp. DLC
Sociological history focusing primarily on the pre-war era.

742. Travis, Fred R. "75´s on Guam." <u>Field Artillery Journal</u>, XXXV (Apr. 1945), pp. 233-234. PCarlMH
Firsthand account of field artillery operations on Guam.

743. Tweed, George R. <u>Robinson Crusoe, U.S.N.: Adventures of George R. Tweed on Jap-held Guam</u>. As told to Blake Clark. New York: McGraw-Hill, 1945. 267 pp. DLC
Account of sailor holding out in the hills during the Japanese occupation of the island.

744. Umezawa, Haruo, and Louis Metzger. "The Defense of Guam." <u>Marine Corps Gazette</u>, XLVIII (Aug. 1964), pp. 36-43. DN
Description of the Japanese defenses of Guam prepared by former Japanese officers.

745. U.S. Navy, Marianas Command. "Permanent Communications and Electronic Facilities, Guam." n.p.: Naval Forces, Oct 1945. 59 pp. ND
Technical report describing the electronic and communications installations on the island.

746. Vanderbreggen, Cornelius, Jr. <u>Letters of a Leatherneck</u>. Laren in Gelderland, the Netherlands: Reapers´ Fellowship Pub., 1948. 290 pp.
Letters of USMCR Lieutenant who participated in the invasion of Guam.

747. Walker, Anthony. "Advance on Orote Peninsula." <u>Marine Corps Gazette</u>, XXIX (Feb. 1945), pp. 8-9. DN
Brief review of battle focusing on the 3nd Battalion, 4th Marines.

748. Williams, J. A. "Guam." <u>All Hands</u>, no. 513 (Oct. 1959), p. 49. DN

8.
Army Air Force Unit Histories

GENERAL

749. Maurer, Maurer, editor. <u>Air Force Combat Units in World War II</u>. Washington: Government Printing Office, 1961. 506 pp. DLC
Comprehensive listing of air forces, commands, air divisions, wings, and groups that were active during WWII providing brief histories, lineages, stations, aircraft used, and commanding officers.

750. _____. <u>Combat Squadrons of the Air Force in World War II</u>. Washington: Government Printing Office, 1969. 841 pp. DLC
Comprehensive listing of squadrons active during the war, including brief histories, lineages, stations, aircraft used, commanding officers.

751. Ravenstein, Charles A. <u>The Organization and Lineage of the United States Air Force</u>. Washington: Office of Air Force History [Government Printing Office], 1986. 77 pp. DLC
Useful compilation of lineages and brief histories of numbered air forces and major combat commands.

AIR FORCES

Seventh Air Force

752. <u>Aloha: Presented by Seventh Air Force</u>. n.p.: ca 1946. 22 lvs. AFHRC
Souvenir pictorial review of operations.

88 THE CENTRAL PACIFIC CAMPAIGN, 1943-1944

753. Howard, Clive, and Joe Whitney. One Damn Island After Another. Chapel Hill, NC: Univ. of North Carolina Press, 1946. 403 pp. AMAU
Comprehensive history of operations including the Central Pacific Campaigns.

754. Olson, James C. Operational History of the Seventh Air Force, 6 November 1943 to 31 July 1944. n.p.: 1945. 248 pp. (USAAF Historical Study, No. 38) AMAU
Narrative history of mid-war operations against Japan.

755. _____ Operational History of the Seventh Air Force, 7 December 1941 to 6 November 1943. n.p.: 1945. 310 pp. (USAAF Historical Study, No. 41) AMAU
Narrative history of early air operations against Japan.

756. Rust, Kenn C. The Seventh Air Force Story...in World War II. Temple City, CA: Historical Aviation Album, 1979. 64 pp. DLC
Brief pictorial history of operations.

757. The Seventh and Eleventh Air Forces in the War Against Japan. Washington: Government Printing Office, 1947. 55 pp. (U.S. Strategic Bombing Survey, Pacific Study No. 70) DAMH
Brief narrative of operations.

758. Fern, Stewart and Lee, editors. Wings Over the Pacific: Seventh Air Force Presented in an Album of Photographs, Its Men and Bases, Its Planes and Targets. Fostoria, OH: Grey Print., 1947. 120 pp.
Pictorial review of operations including the Central Pacific campaign.

Twentieth Air Force

759. Birdsall, Steve. Saga of the Superfortress: The Dramatic Story of the B-29 and the Twentieth Air Force. Garden City: Doubleday, 1980. 346 pp. AMAU
Pictorial history of B-29 operations in the 20th Air Force.

760. Bozung, Jack H., editor. The 20th Over Japan. Los Angeles: AAF Pub. Co., 1946. 40 lvs. AMAU
Pictorial history.

761. Cate, James L. History of the Twentieth Air Force: Genesis. n.p.: 1945. 298 pp. (USAAF Historical Study, No. 112) AMAU
Comprehensive narrative history of operations.

762. Finkelstein, N. Memorial Album: Dedicated to the Boys of the 20th Air Force. Los Angeles: Economy Typesetting Service, 1951. 134 pp. AMAU
Memorial album of letters from an airman.

763. Gurney, Gene. Journey of the Giants. New York: Coward-McCann, 1964. 280 pp. AMAU
History of B-29 operations with the 20th Air Force.

ARMY AIR FORCE UNIT HISTORIES   89

764. Hansell, Heywood S., Jr. Strategic Air War Against Japan. Washington: Government Printing Office, 1980. 151 pp. AMAU
Comprehensive history of the 20th Air Force operations by one of its early commanders.

765. Highlights of the 20th Air Force, Prepared by the Personnel Narratives Division, Office of Information Services, Headquarters, Army Air Forces. New York: 1945. 9 pp. Mimeo NN
Brief narrative history.

766. Keenan, Richard M. Resume 20th Air Force Missions. Washington: 1969. 387 pp. CoCA
Comprehensive listing of 20th Air Force missions.

767. _____ The 20th Air Force Album. Washington: 20th Air Force Assn., 1982. 284 pp.
Pictorial history of operations.

768. Marshall, Chester. Sky Giants Over Japan, a Diary of a B-29 Crew in WWII. Memphis, TN: Marshall Pubs., 1984. 214 pp. DLC
History from the perspective a of bomber crew member.

769. _____, editor. The Global Twentieth: An Anthology of the 20th AF in WWII. Vol. 1. Winona, MN: Apollo Books, 1985.

770. Morrison, Wilbur H. Point of No Return: The Story of the Twentieth Air Force. New York: Times Books, 1979. 279 pp. AMAU
Popular history of the 20th Air Force.

771. Murphy, Charles J. V. "The Air War on Japan." Fortune, XXXII (Sept. 1945), pp. 117-123; and (Oct. 1945), pp. 132-137. DLC
Review of the deployment and campaigns of the Twentieth Air Force.

772. Rust, Kenn C. Twentieth Air Force Story...in World War II. Temple City, CA: Historical Aviation Album, 1979. 64 pp. AMAU
Pictorial history of operations.

773. Sinclair, William B. The Big Brothers: The Story of the B-29´s. San Antonio, TX: Naylor, 1972. 132 pp. AMAU
Pictorial history of B-29 operations in the 20th Air Force.

774. Synder, Earl A. General Leemy´s Circus: A Navigator´s Story of the 20th Air Force. New York: Exposition Press, 1955. 175 pp. AMAU
Account from the perspective of a B-29 crew member.

775. The Strategic Air Operations of Very Heavy Bombardment in the War Against Japan (Twentieth Air Force), Final Report. Washington: Government Printing Office, 1946. 41 pp. (U.S. Strategic Bombing Survey, Pacific Study No. 66) DAMH
Brief history of operations.

776. Twining, Nathan F. "The Twentieth Air Force." Military Review, XXVI (June 1946), pp. 65-69. PCarlMH
Review of its activities by its former commander.

777. Twentieth Air Force: A Statistical Summary of Its Operations Against Japan. n.p.: ca1945. 92 pp. AFHRC
Series of charts depicting operational statistics and information.

778. U.S. Army Air Force, Twentieth Air Force. Starvation. n.p.: Air Force, 56 pp. DN
Account of the operations staged from the Marianas bases on the Japanese Islands.

779. Wolfe, Kenneth B. "The Men of the B-29's." Air Force, XXVII (Sept. 1944), pp. 4-8, 44. PCarlMH
Review by a commander of the units that bombed Japan.

COMMANDS

21st Bomber Command

780. Boyle, James M. "The XXI Bomber Command: Primary Factor in the Defeat of Japan." unpublished Ph.D dissertation, St. Louis Univ., 1964. 254 pp.
Comprehensive review of operations against Japan from bases in the Marianas.

781. _____ _____ Aerospace Historian, XI (Apr. 1966), pp. 44-53.
PCarlMH
Brief history.

GROUPS

3rd Bombardment Group

782. Cortesi, Lawrence. The Grim Reapers. History of the 3rd Bomb Group, 1918-1965. Temple City, CA: Historical Aviation Album, 1985. 105 pp. DLC
Pictorial history of B-25 operations including attacks on Rabaul in support of the Central Pacific drive.

783. The Reaper's Harvest, the Story of the Third Attack Group. Sydney: Halstead Press, 1945. 120 pp. AFHRC
Pictorial history of operations including attacks on Rabaul in support of the Central Pacific drive. Awards and killed in action listed.

6th Bombardment Group

784. Rice, W. M., editor. Pirate's Log: A Historical Record of the Sixth Bombardment Group. Manila: 2771st Engr. Base Reproduction Co., 1946. 71 pp. NN
Pictorial history of operations of B-29 unit stationed on Tinian. Killed in Action listed.

9th Bombardment Group

785. War Journal. Ninth Bombardment Group, United States Army Air Forces. n.p.: 947th Engr. Avn. Topo. Co., ca1945. 15 lvs.
Brief history of B-29 unit stationed on Tinian.

11th Bombardment Group

786. Cleveland, W. M. Grey Geese Calling: Pacific Air War History of the 11th Bombardment Group Heavy in the Pacific, 1940-1945. Askow, MN: American Pub. Co., 1981. 492 pp. AMAU
Pictorial history of a B-24 unit including operations against the Gilberts, Marshalls, and the Marianas.

787. _____. Planes' Names: A Listing of the Planes' Names (and Serial Numbers, where known) for Combat Aircraft of the 11th Bombardment Group (H) From Hawaii Down the Pacific to the Solomon Islands, and From Guadalcanal to Okinawa in the Far Pacific. Portsmouth, NH: 11th Bombardment Group (H) Assn., 1977. 100 pp. DLC
Pictorial history focusing on the unit's aircraft.

39th Bombardment Group

788. Palmer, Bernard. Dangerous Mission. Grand Rapids: Zoneran Pub. House, 1945. 58 pp. DLC
Brief history of a B-29 unit stationed on Guam.

40th Bombardment Group

789. Eustis, Lawrence B., editor. 40th Bombardment Group, a Pictorial Record of Events, Places and People in India, China and Tinian, From April, 1944, Through October, 1945... San Angelo, TX: Newsfoto Pub. Co., 1946. 141 lvs. AMAU
Pictorial history of a B-29 unit stationed on Tinian with a Unit Roster.

790. McGregor, Carter. The Kagu-Tsuchi Bomb Group. Wichita Falls, KS: Nortex Press, 1981. 226 pp. TxWicM

41st Bombardment Group

791. Ellison, Lee, and others, editors. The Forty First Service Record. The Purpose of this Book is to Recapture Once More, if only for a Fleeting Moment, the Tears and Laughter, the Heartache and Fun of Over Two Years of Overseas Service... n.p.: 1945. 45 lvs.
Pictorial history of operations including those against Tarawa and the Marshalls. Unit Roster and those killed in action listed.

330th Bombardment Group

792. 330th Bomb Group Digest. n.p.: 947th Engr. Avn. Topo. Co., 1946.
Brief history of operations of B-29 unit stationed on Guam in early 1945.

331st Bombardment Group

793. The 331st Bombardment Group (VH) from Activation until V-J Day. Guam: 947th Engr. Avn. Co., ca1945. 14 lvs.
Brief history of operations of B-29 unit stationed on Guam in mid-1945.

345th Bombardment Group

794. Blount, R. E. Preppy. We Band of Brothers. Austin, TX: Eakin Press, 1984. 393 pp. CtMan

795. Hanna, John C., and William R. Witherell, Jr., editors. Warpath [of the] Air Apaches: The Story of the 345th Bombardment Group in World War II. San Angelo, TX: Newsfoto Pub. Co., 1946. 277 pp. [22] pp. AMAU
Pictorial history of B-25 unit, including operations against Rabaul in support of the Central Pacific drive. Unit roster provided.

796. Hickey, Lawrence J. Warpath Across the Pacific: The Illustrated History of the 345th Bombardment Group During World War II. Boulder, CO: International Pub. Corp., 1984. 448 pp. KWi
Pictorial history concentrating primarily on the Southwest Pacific operations

444th Bombardment Group

797. The Pictorial History of the 444th Bombardment Group, Very Heavy Special. San Angelo, TX: Newsfoto Pub. Co., 1945. 80 lvs. DLC
Pictorial history of a B-29 unit stationed on Tinian with Unit Roster.

ARMY AIR FORCE UNIT HISTORIES 93

468th Bombardment Group

798. Wolfe, Stephen, editor. The Story of the "Billy Mitchell" Group: 468th H-Bomb Group from the CBI to the Marianas. n.p.: 1946. 135 pp.
Pictorial history of operations of B-29 unit stationed on Tinian in early 1945.

494th Bombardment Group

799. Williams, Jack J., and others. 494th Bomb Group History. Philadelphia: W. T. Peck and Co., 1947. 147 pp. NN
Pictorial history of 7th Air Force B-24 unit, including Central Pacific campaign support missions.

497th Bombardment Group

800. Goforth, Pat. E., editor. The Long Haul, the Story of the 497th Bomb Group (VH). San Angelo, TX: Newsfoto Pub. Co., 1946. 124 lvs. AMAU
Pictorial history of operations of B-29 unit stationed on Saipan from mid-1944. Unit Roster and those killed in action listed.

498th Bombardment Group

801. 498th Bombardment Group Presents Its Combat Story: 20 November 1943 to 15 August 1945. n.p.: ca1945. 157 pp. PP
Pictorial history of operations of B-29 unit stationed on Saipan in early 1945.

499th Bombardment Group

802. Burkett, Prentiss. The Unofficial History of the 499th Bomb Group (VH). Temple City, CA: Historical Aviation Album, 1981. 56 pp. DLC
Pictorial history of operations of B-29 unit stationed on Saipan in mid-1944.

500th Bombardment Group

803. McClure, Glenn E., editor. An Unofficial History of the 500th Bombardment Group, One of Four Combat Groups in the 73rd Wing under 21st Bomber Command and 20th Air Force, Stationed for Overseas Operation at Saipan in the Marianas Islands. Riverside, CA: Rubidoux Print. Co., 1946. 100 lvs. NN
Pictorial history of operations of B-29 unit stationed on Saipan in late 1944. Unit Roster and those killed in action listed.

504th Bombardment Group

804. Combat Diary: A Record of the 504th Bombardment Group. n.p.: 949th Engr. Avn. Topo Co., 1946. 12 lvs. NN
Brief history of operations of B-29 unit stationed on Tinian in early 1945.

805. Midlam, Don S. Flight of the Lucky Lady. Portland, OR: Binfords & Mort Pubs., ca1954. 208 pp. DLC

505th Bombardment Group

806. MacIntyre, Becky, editor. The 505th Bombardment Group, 1944-1945. A Report from the 484th Bomb Squadron. n.p.: Becky MacIntyre, n.d. 74 pp.
Brief history of operations of B-29 unit stationed on Tinian in late 1944.

509th Composite Group

807. Marx, Joseph L. Seven Hours to Zero. New York: G. P. Putnam's Sons, 1967. 256 pp. DLC

808. Ossip, Jerome J., editor. 509th Pictorial Album... Chicago: Rogers Print. Co., 1946. 56 lvs. AFHRC
Pictorial history of the B-29 unit that dropped the atomic bombs on Japan. Group photographs with personnel identified.

809. Thomas, Gordon, and Max M. Witts. Enola Gay. New York: Stein and Day Pubs., 1977. 327 pp. DLC
Popular history of the bomb crew and unit that dropped the first atomic bomb on Japan.

SQUADRONS

8th Radio Squadron

810. The Story Behind the Flying Eight-Ball. n.p.: ca1945. 99 pp.
Informal history of a radio intelligence unit including its service on Guam.

19th Fighter Squadron

811. 19th Tactical Fighter Sq. History, 1917-1945. Dallas, TX: Taylor Pub. Co., 1985. 128 pp. DLC
Pictorial history of operations of a P-38 unit stationed on Saipan with the 318th Fighter Group.

ARMY AIR FORCE UNIT HISTORIES   95

56th Depot Repair Squadron

812. Dedication. To the Men of the 56th Depot Repair Squadron, the Few Who Taught So Many the Meaning of Service, This History is Dedicated. Guam: 1945. 34 lvs. PCarlMH
Review of a service unit including its service on Guam.

873rd Bombardment Squadron

813. Kroesen, Paul, editor. The 873rd Bombardment Squadron Presents Superfort Saga, History of the First and the Finest B-29 Squadron in the Marianas Islands. Buena Park, CA: West Orange County Pub. Co., 1946. 96 pp. AMAU
Pictorial history of operations of a B-29 unit stationed on Saipan with 498th Bomb Group. Unit Roster and those killed in action listed.

MISCELLANEOUS UNITS

1st Aircraft Repair Unit (Floating)

814. The Odyssey of the 1st ARU (F)... Chicago: Inland Press, 1946. 73 lvs. AFHRC

9.
Army Unit Histories

DIVISIONS

General

815. Army Times, editors of. Combat Divisions of World War II (Army of the United States). Washington: Army Times, 1946. 96 pp. DLC
Provides very brief histories of each of the divisions to see service in WWII, including the 7th Infantry, 27th and 77th Infantry Division.

816. Jacobs, Bruce. Soldiers, the Fighting Divisions of the Regular Army. New York: W. W. Norton, 1958. 367 pp. DLC
Compilation of brief histories of the various Regular Army divisions including the 7th Infantry Division.

817. Kahn, Ely J., and Henry McLemore. Fighting Divisions. Washington: Infantry Journal Press, 1945. 218 pp. DLC
Provides a one-page popular history of each division including the 7th, 27th and 77th Infantry divisions.

818. Wilson, John B. Army Lineage Series, Armies, Corps, Divisions and Separate Brigades. Washington: Government Printing Office, 1987. 736 pp. (Army Lineage Series) PCarlMH
Comprehensive review of the structure and history of the Army tactical divisions and corps, plus a brief history, lineages and honors received for each unit.

7th Infantry Division

819. 7th Infantry Division--Flintlock Operation, Field Orders and Report of Operation. Fort Leavenworth: Command & General Staff College, 1944. 153 pp.
Compilation of orders and after-action reports.

820. Arnold, A. V. Flintlock Operation, Southern Force Artillery.
n.p.: HQ, 7th Infantry Div., 1944. 18 pp. ART
Review of 7th Division Artillery operations during the battle for
Kwajalein.

821. Marshall, Samuel L. A. Island Victory, the Battle of Kwajalein
Atoll. Washington: Infantry Journal Press, 1945. 117 pp. PCarlMH
Contemporary narrative of the battle compiled from interviews of
veterans of the battle.

822. Love, Edmond G. The Hourglass, a History of the 7th Infantry
Division in World War II. Washington: Infantry Journal Press, 1950.
496 pp. PCarlMH
Most complete history of the division's activities during WWII.

27th Infantry Division

823. The Capture of Makin. Washington: Government Print. Office,
1946. 136 pp. [American Forces in Action Series, no. 10.] PCarlMH
Detailed history of 27th Infantry Division in the battle to capture
Makin.

824. Gailey, Harry A. Howlin' Mad Smith vs. the Army. Conflict in
Command, Saipan 1944. Novato, CA: Presidio Press, 1986. 278 pp.
PCarlMH
Detailed review of the events leading up to and after the relief of MG
Ralph Smith, USA. by LTG Holland Smith, USMC on Saipan.

825. Love, Edmond G. The 27th Infantry Division in World War II.
Washington: Infantry Journal Press, 1949. 677 pp. PCarlMH
(reprinted by Battery Press, 1981.)
Most complete history of the division's activities during WWII.

826. _____ "OMAK." Army, XXXI (Sept. 1981). pp. 37+. PCarlMH
Account of Captain Arthur Klein, USA.

827. _____ "The 27th's Battle for Saipan." Infantry Journal, LIX
(Sept. 1946), pp. 8-17. PCarlMH
Detailed account of division's operations.

828. Pictorial History Twenty-seventh Division, United States Army,
1940-41. Atlanta, GA: Army Navy Pub. Co., 1941. PCarlMH
Pre-war pictorial history of the training activities; contains unit
and officer photographs.

829. Report of Canadian Officers Attached to 27th Infantry Division,
United States Army, for the Saipan Operation. APO 958: 1944. 60
pp. Typescript PCarlMH

ARMY UNIT HISTORIES 99

830. Small Unit Actions. (The Fight for Tanapag Plain, pp. 65-113). Washington: Government Printing Office, 1946. [American Forces in Action Series, No. 11.] PCarlMH
Detailed history of the 27th Infantry Division operations on the Tanapag Plain on Saipan.

77th Infantry Division

831. Bruce, Andrews D. "Administration, Supply, and Evacuation of the 77th Infantry Division on Guam." Military Review, XXIV (Dec. 1944). pp. 3-12. PCarlMH
Division's commander review of the operation and insights to command decisions.

832. Gabrynowicz, Elizabeth. "Tough 'Old' Guys." Soldiers, XXXXI (Apr. 1986), pp. 34-36. DLC
General brief account of operations including the Central Pacific operations.

833. Guam Operations of the 77th Division. Washington: Government Printing Office, 1946. 136 pp. (American Forces in Action Series, no. 9) PCarlMH
Detailed history of the 77th Infantry Division operations in the capture of Guam.

834. Ours to Hold High. The History of the 77th Infantry Division in World War II. Washington: Infantry Journal Press, 1947. 585 pp. PCarlMH
Most complete history of the division's activities during WWII.

INFANTRY REGIMENTS

General

835. The Army Lineage Book. Volume II: Infantry. Washington: Government Printing Office, 1955. 859 pp. PCarlMH
Compilation of brief histories and lineages for each infantry regiment including national guard and army reserve units.

836. Mahon, John K., and Romana Danysh. Infantry. Part 1, Regular Army. Washington: Office of the Chief of Military History [Government Printing Office], 1972. 938 pp. (Army Lineage Series) PCarlMH
Updated edition of the above entry for regular army regiments only.

837. Sawicki, James A. Infantry Regiments of the U.S. Army. Dumfries, VA: Wyvern Pubs., 1981. 682 pp. PCarlMH
Compilation of lineages and honors for each infantry regiment, includes organic unit tables for WWII.

838. Waltham, Melvin C. *We Can't All Be Heroes. A History of Separate Infantry Regiments in World War II.* Hicksville, NY: Exposition Press, 1975. 159 pp. PCarlMH
Provides short histories of each separate regiment, including the 111th Infantry which served in the Marshalls.

17th Infantry Regiment

839. *Historical and Pictorial Review of the Seventeenth Infantry, Seventh Division, United States Army, Fort Ord, California.* Baton Rouge: Army Navy Pub. Co., 1941.
Pre-war pictorial of training activities; contains unit and officer photographs.

840. Marshall, Samuel L. A. "Action in the Pigpen." *Infantry Journal*, LV (Nov. 1944), pp. 39-47. PCarlMH
Account of 1st Battalion on Ebeye Island.

32nd Infantry Regiment

841. "Kwajalein Day by Day." *Infantry Journal*, LV (Aug. 1944), pp. 12-13. PCarlMH
Series of daily maps showing progress made.

842. _____. "Men Against Darkness." *Infantry Journal*, LV (Dec. 1944), pp. 43-51. PCarlMH
Critique of Company C in Kwajalein operations.

843. _____. "Ordeal by Fire." *Infantry Journal*, LV (Oct. 1944), pp. 35-44. PCarlMH
Critique of actions on Kwajalein.

165th Infantry Regiment

844. Jenkins, Burris. *Father Meany and the Fighting 69th (Fighting Irish) 69th of New York--165th U.S. Infantry.* New York: Frederick Fell, Inc., 1944. 61 pp. PCarlMH
Narrative suffering from lack of detail due to wartime censorship concerning a Catholic chaplain with the regiment on Makin.

184th Infantry Regiment

845. *184th Infantry, Camp San Luis Obispo, 1941.* Baton Rouge: Army Navy Pub. Co., 1941. 131 pp. PCarlMH
Pre-war pictorial history of training activities; contains unit and officer photographs.

846. Marshall, Samuel L. A. "Fight to the Finish." *Infantry Journal*, LVI (Jan. 1945), pp. 45-52. PCarlMH
Account of 2nd Battalion on Kwajalein.

ARMY UNIT HISTORIES 101

305th Infantry Regiment

847. Donnelly, Thomas J. "Hey Padre." The Saga of a Regimental Chaplain in World War II. New York: 77th Division Association, 1986. 132 pp.
Memoirs of the regimental chaplain including service on Guam.

848. West, Charles O. Second to None! The Story of the 305th Infantry in World War II. Washington: Infantry Journal Press, 1949. 243 pp. PCarlMH
Most complete history including operations on Guam.

306th Infantry Regiment

849. Davis, Sumner D. Dear Folks, a Series of Letters. Birmingham: 1945. Mimeo PCarlMH
Compilation of letters from a GI with the 306th Infantry.

307th Infantry Regiment

850. Lopez, Henry D. From Jackson to Japan, the History of Company C, 307th, 77th Division, in World War II. n.p.: 1977. 247 pp. PCarlMH
Detailed history of company including operations on Guam.

ARTILLERY UNITS

General

851. McKenney, Janice E. Air Defense Artillery. Washington: Government Printing Office, 1985. 489 pp. (Army Lineage Series) PCarlMH
Compilation of lineages of the current Air Defense Regiments and their antecedent units including some who served in the Central Pacific.

852. _____ Field Artillery, Regular Army and Army Reserve. Washington: Government Printing Office, 1985. 761 pp. (Army Lineage Series) PCarlMH
Compilation of lineages of the current Field Artillery Regiments and their antecedent units including some who served in the Central Pacific.

853. Sawicki, James A. Field Artillery Battalions of World War II. Dumfries, VA: Centaur Pubs., 1977. 2 vols. PCarlMH
Compilation of field artillery battalion lineages plus divisional organic unit tables for WWII.

7th AntiAircraft Battalion

854. A History of the 7th Anti Aircraft Artillery Automatic Weapons Battalion. n.p.: 1945. Mimeo
Battalion served on Guam.

304th Field Artillery Battalion

855. Members of Headquarters Battery, 304th Field Artillery Battalion, 77th Division, World War No. 2. Philadelphia: David S. Brown, Printer, 1945. 20 pp.
Roster of the HQ battery, organic to the 77th Infantry Division.

856. "A History of the 304th Field Artillery Battalion, World War II." The Pirate's Piece, 304th F.A., XXXII (Nov. 1952).
Battalion served with 77th Infantry Division on Guam.

305th Field Artillery Battalion

857. Kadar, Alfred F., editor. 305th Field Artillery Battalion, 77th Infantry Division. Hakodate: Dai-Ichi Insatsu, 1946. 72 pp. PCarlMH
Brief history including the Guam operations.

CAVALRY & ARMOR UNITS

General

858. Sawicki, James A. Tank Battalion of the U.S. Army. Dumfries, VA: Wyvern Pub., 1986. 427 pp. PCarlMH
Compilation of lineages, includes a table of battalions that were attached or organic to divisions during the war.

77th Reconnaissance Troop

859. Bridgewater, F. Clay. "Reconnaissance on Guam." The Cavalry Journal, LIV (May-June 1945), pp. 46-48. PCarlMH
Author was commanding officer of Troop on Guam; provides a brief review of training, equipment, and operations.

ENGINEER UNITS

13th Engineer Battalion

860. Engineer Pictorial Report of the 7th Infantry Division Amphibious Invasion of Kwajalein Island. Kwajalein: 1944. 50 pp. PCarlMH
A pictorial history of the engineer aspects of the Kwajalein operation.

ARMY UNIT HISTORIES

47th Engineer Construction Battalion

861. 47, "Our Record," A History of the Forty-seventh Engineer Construction Battalion. Okinawa: 1945-46. 2 vols. Mimeo
Provided garrison troops for Eniwetok.

50th Engineer Combat Battalion

862. Lorber, Donald L., editor. 50th Engineer Combat Battalion. n.p.: 69th Engr. Topo. Co., 1945. 52 pp. PCarlMH
Participated in the Kwajalein operation.

64th Engineer Battalion

863. 64th Operational Report. n.p.: n.d. 32 lvs. ViFbe

864. This Outfit, These Men. n.p.: 1945. 114 lvs. NN
Served on Guam.

233rd Engineer Combat Battalion

865. Weaver, Victor E. The 233d Engineer Combat Battalion, 1943-1945. Washington: Infantry Journal Press, 1947. 160 pp. PCarlMH
Supported Guam operations, including shore party, road construction and maintenance activities.

242nd Engineer Battalion

866. South Dakota in World War II. Pierre, SD: World War II History Commission, n.d. 698 pp. DLC
"242nd Engineer Battalion," pp. 390-3, by John J. Steele, includes operations on Guam.

AVIATION ENGINEER UNITS

933rd Engineer Aviation Regiment

867. "Pacific Duty with the 933rd" Engr. Avn. Regt. H. M. Co. n.p.: n.d. 76 pp.
Served on Guam.

805th Engineer Aviation Battalion

868. Marleau, Thomas J. Bulldozers and Bombers: A History of the 805th Engineer Avn. Bn., 1941-1961. Baldwinsville, NY: Thomas J. Marleau, 1981. 316 pp. CoCA
Pictorial history including service on Saipan.

854th Engineer Aviation Battalion

869. <u>Mission Completed. The Pictorial History of the 854th Aviation Engineers from 1 January 1943 to 2 September 1945</u>. San Francisco: James H. Barry Co., ca1945. 130 pp.
Served on Guam.

1885th Engineer Aviation Battalion

870. <u>The ´85 Moves Up. 1885th Engr. Avn. Bn.</u> n.p.: 933rd Engr. Avn. Regt., ca1945. 12 lvs.
Served on Guam.

1886th Engineer Aviation Battalion

871. <u>History of the 1886th</u>. n.p.: ca1945.
Served on Guam.

1887th Engineer Aviation Battalion

872. <u>The 1887th Engineer Aviation Battalion</u>. n.p.: 927th Engr. Avn. Regt., 1945. 80 pp. NN
Served on Guam.

903rd Engineer Air Force HQ Company

873. <u>Remember When?</u> n.p.: ca1945. ca100 lvs. AFHRC

904th Engineer Air Force HQ Company

874. <u>Memories. Reproduction Platoon 904th Engineer Air Force Headquarters Company</u>. n.p.: 904th Engr. A.F. HQ Co., 1945. 53 pp. [26] lvs.

MISCELLANEOUS UNITS

Central Pacific Base Command

875. <u>History of the Central Pacific Base Command During World War II, 1 July 1944 - 2 September 1945</u>. n.p.: ca1945. CMH
Administrative history of command.

U.S. Army Forces, Middle Pacific Command

876. U.S. Army Forces, Middle Pacific Command. History of Army Port and Service Command. n.p.: HQ, Army Forces, Middle Pacific, 1947. 186 pp. ND
History from August 1943 through June 1946, lists both personnel and facilities.

877. _____ History of the Area Artillery Office, Headquarters, Army Forces Middle Pacific (25 January 1942 to 15 October). n.p.: 1945. 127 pp. PCarlMH

878. _____ Organizational Charts from the Pacific. n.p.: Historical Bureau, U.S. Army Forces, Middle Pacific, 1945. 17 pp. PCarlMH

879. Your Victory. n.p.: ca1945. 46 lvs.
Brief souvenir history of the command activites during the war.

10.
Marine Corps Unit Histories

GROUND UNITS

DIVISIONS

880. McMillan, George, and others. <u>Uncommon Valor: Marine Divisions in Action</u>. Washington: Infantry Journal Press, 1946. 256 pp. DN
Review of the Marine Divisions in the War, plus an essay on each of the six Marine Divisions.

2nd Marine Division

881. Johnson, Richard W. <u>Follow Me. The Story of the Second Marine Division in World War II</u>. New York: Random House, 1948. 305 pp. DN
Comprehensive history of the division including operations on Tarawa and Guam.

882. Silcox, S. G. <u>A Hillbilly Marine</u>. n.p.: privately printed, 1977. 176 pp.
Personal narrative, author served with the division on Saipan.

883. Zimmerman, John L. <u>Second Marine Division</u>. Washington: Historical Division, HQ, US Marine Corps, 1945. 24 lvs. DN
Brief outline history of the division's operations, including its participation in the Gilbert and Marianas invasions.

3rd Marine Division

884. Arthur, Robert A., and Kenneth Cohlmia. The Third Marine Division. Washington: Infantry Journal Press, 1948. 399 pp. DN
Comprehensive history including operations on Guam.

885. Conner, John. "Enter the 3rd Marine Division." Marine Corps Gazette, XXVIII (July 1945), pp. 15-17. DN
Brief review.

886. Josephy, Alvin M., Jr. The Long and the Short and the Tall: The Story of a Marine Combat Unit in the Pacific. New York: Knopf, 1946. 221 pp. DN
Detailed history including operations on Guam.

887. Letcher, John S. One Marine's Story. Verona, VA: McClure Press, 1970. 387 pp. DLC
Author served with the 3rd Marine Division Artillery.

888. Thacker, Joel D. "History of the 3rd Division." Leatherneck, XXIX (Feb. 1946), pp. 12-15+. DN
Brief history of operations.

889. Third Marine Division and Its Regiments. Washington: Historical Division, HQ, U.S.M.C., 1983. 61 pp. DN
Brief history of the division and the 4th, 9th, 12th, 21st, 26th Marine Regiments, including commanding officers, lineages, honors.

4th Marine Division

890. Chaplin, John C. The Fourth Marine Division in World War II. Washington: Historical Division, HQ, US Marine Corps, 1945. DN
Comprehensive history including operations in the Marshalls and Marianas.

891. _____. "History of the 4th Marine Division." Leatherneck, XXIX (Apr. 1946), pp. 20-21+. DN
Brief history of operations.

892. Fourth Marine Division, United States Marine Corps. Camp Joseph H. Pendleton, CA: 1943.
Pictorial review of the division training at Camp Pendleton.

893. A Pocket History of the 4th Marine Division and the 4th Marine Aircraft Wing in World War II. n.p.: Government Printing Office, 1965. DLC
Brief pictorial history of operations.

894. Proehl, Carl W. The Fourth Marine Division in World War II. Washington: Infantry Journal Press, 1946. 238 pp. DN
Comprehensive history of the division.

MARINE CORPS UNIT HISTORIES 109

895. Service Troops, 4th Marine Division. Baton Rouge: Army & Navy Pub. Co., ca1942.
Pictorial history of troops in training.

896. Thomason, John W., 3rd. "The Fourth Marine Division at Tinian." Marine Corps Gazette, XXIX (Jan. 1945), pp. 2-9. DN
Detailed account of division's operations.

897. U.S. Marine Corps. Fourth Marine Division Operations Report: Tinian, 24 July to 1 August 1944. n.p.: HQ, 4th Marine Division, 1944. 153 pp. PCarlMH
After action report of division's operations.

REGIMENTS

2nd Marine Regiment

898. Johnstone, John H. A Brief History of the 2d Marines. Washington: Historical Branch, G-3 Division, HQ, U.S. Marine Corps, 1961. 14 pp. (Marine Corps Historical Reference Series, no. 32.) DN
Brief history including operations in the Gilberts and Marianas with the 2nd Marine Division.

3rd Marine Regiment

899. Benis, Frank M. A Brief History of the 3rd Marines. Washington: Historical Branch, G-3 Division, HQ, U.S. Marine Corps, 1961. 18 pp. (Marine Corps Historical Reference Series, no. 35) DN
Brief history including operations on Guam with 3rd Marine Division.

4th Marine Regiment

900. Condit, Kenneth W., and Edwin T. Turnbladh. Hold High the Torch. A History of the 4th Marines. Washington: Historical Branch, G-3 Division, HQ, U.S. Marine Corps, 1960. 330 pp. DN
Comprehensive history including operations on Makin with 6th Marine Division.

901. Ringler, Jack K. A Brief History of the 4th Marines. Washington: Historical Branch, G-3 Division, U.S. Marine Corps, 1969. DN
Brief history of regiment.

6th Marine Regiment

902. Jones, William K. A Brief History of the 6th Marines. Washington: History and Museums Division, HQ, U.S.M.C, 1987. 191 pp. DN
Comprehensive history including operations on Tarawa and Saipan-Tinian with 2nd Marine Division.

110 THE CENTRAL PACIFIC CAMPAIGN, 1943-1944

8th Marine Regiment

903. Hammel, Eric M., and John E. Lane. "1st Battalion, 8th Marines at Tarawa." Marine Corps Gazette, LXVII (Nov. 1983), pp. 84-91. DN
Comments on command and communications problems during the invasion; served with 2nd Marine Division.

904. Santelli, James S. A Brief History of the 8th Marines. Washington: History & Museum Division, HQ, U.S. Marine Corps, 1976. 103 pp. DN
Brief history including operations on Tarawa and Saipan-Tinian.

9th Marine Regiment

905. Hendryx, Gene. Semper Fi! The Story of the 9th Marines. New York: Pageant Press, 1959. 370 pp. DLC
History of the regiment including service on Guam with the 3rd Marine Division.

906. Burris, L. D., editor. The Ninth Marines, a Brief History of the Ninth Marine Regiment. Washington: Infantry Journal Press, 1946. 375 pp. DN
Comprehensive history of operations including those on Guam.

907. Strobridge, Truman R. A Brief History of the 9th Marines. Washington: Historical Branch, G-3 Division, HQ, U.S. Marine Corps, 1961. 12 pp. (Marine Corps Historical Reference Series, no. 33.) DN
Brief history including operations on Guam.

12th Marine Regiment

908. Smith, Charles R. A Brief History of the 12th Marines. Washington: History and Museums Division, HQ, U.S.M.C, 1972. DN
Brief history including participation on Guam with the 3rd Marine Division.

21st Marine Regiment

909. Kaufman, Millard, "Attack on Guam." Marine Corps Gazette, XXIX (Apr. 1945), pp. 2-5. DN
Author served with 21st Marines and participated in the Guam operation with the 3rd Marine Division.

24th Marine Regiment

910. Stott, Frederic A. Saipan Under Fire. Andover, MA: 1945. 13 pp. DN
Actions of 1st battalion of the regiment with the 4th Marine Division.

MARINE CORPS UNIT HISTORIES   111

911. <u>24th Regiment, 4th Marine Division</u>. Baton Rouge: Army Navy Pub. Co., ca1942.
Photographic history of the regiment in training.

25th Marine Regiment

912. Ruth, Joseph B. <u>A Brief History of the 25th Marines</u>. Washington: History and Museums Division, HQ, U.S.M.C, 1981. 60 pp. DN
Part of 4th Marine Division, participated in the Tinian invasion.

913. <u>25th Regiment, 4th Marine Division</u>. Baton Rouge: Army Navy Pub. Co., ca1942.
Photographic history of the regiment in training.

MARINE ARTILLERY UNITS

10th Marine Regiment

914. Buckner, David N. <u>A Brief History of the 10th Marines</u>. Washington: History and Museums Division, HQ, U.S.M.C., 1981. 131 pp. DN
Comprehensive history including operations with the 2nd Marine Division on Tarawa and Saipan-Tinian.

915. Jenkins, J. C. "The Tenth Marines." <u>Marine Corps Gazette</u>, XXVI (Apr. 1943), p. 37. DN
Brief review.

14th Marine Regiment

916. <u>14th Regiment, 4th Marine Division</u>. Baton Rouge: Army Navy Pub. Co., ca1942.
Photographic history of the regiment in training.

2nd 155mm Howitzer Battalion

917. Miller, William. "The Forgotten Battalion." <u>Leatherneck</u>, XXVIII (Feb. 1945), pp. 15-17. DN
Review of service at Tarawa, Eniwetok, Saipan, and Guam.

MARINE ENGINEERS UNITS

20th Marine Regiment (Engineers)

918. <u>20th Regiment, 4th Marine Division</u>. Baton Rouge: Army Navy Pub. Co., ca1942.
Photographic history of the regiment in training.

112   THE CENTRAL PACIFIC CAMPAIGN, 1943-1944

MISCELLANEOUS MARINE UNITS

3rd Amphibious Tractor Battalion

919. Miller, Ben. "The Boys from Alligator Flats." *Leatherneck*, XXVIII (Aug. 1945), pp. 35+. DN
Operations on Guam.

3rd Medical Battalion

920. Callaway, Raymond R. "The Third Medical Battalion in Action: Bougainville and Guam." unpublished paper, Historical Study, Marine Corps Schools Senior Course, 1948-49. n.p.: 1949.
Brief history of 3rd Marine Division's organic medical battalion.

921. Updegraph, Charles L., Jr. *U.S. Marine Corps Special Units of World War II*. Washington: Historical Division, HQ, U.S.M.C., 1972. 105 pp. (Historical Reference Pamphlet) DN
Includes brief history of 5th Defense Battalion in the Gilberts.

MARINE AVIATION

Marine Attack Squadron 311

922. Sambito, William J. *History of Marine Attack Squadron 311*. Washington: History and Museums Division, HQ, U.S.M.C., 1978. 67 pp. DN
Includes operations in the Marshalls.

11.
Naval Unit Histories

AIRCRAFT CARRIERS

USS Barnes, CVE 20

923. <u>Cruise of the U.S.S. Barnes, 1943-1945</u>. San Francisco: Knight-Counihan Co., 1945. 40 lvs.
Pictorial history including the transporting of aircraft and personnel; and as a combat training and pilot qualifying ship, bombed Tarawa as part of these duties in Nov-Dec 1943.

USS Bataan, CVL 29

924. <u>The U.S.S. Bataan, 1 August 1943-17 October 1945</u>. Charlotte, NC: Observer Print. House, 1946. 218 pp.
Pictorial history including the invasion of Saipan, and the Battle of the Philippine Sea.

USS Belleau Woods, CVL 24

925. <u>Flight Quarters: The War Story of the U.S.S. Belleau Woods, Aircraft Carrier</u>. Los Angeles: Cole-Holmquist Press, 1946. 189 pp.
Pictorial history including the operations in the Kwajalein and Majuro Atolls, and Saipan. Ship's aircraft credited with sinking Japanese Carrier Hiyo in the Battle of the Philippine Sea.

114 THE CENTRAL PACIFIC CAMPAIGN, 1943-1944

USS Bunker Hill, CV 17

926. The U.S.S. Bunker Hill, November 1943 - November 1944: The Record of a Carrier's Combat Action Against the Axis Nations in the Pacific. Chicago: Rogers Print. Co., 1944. 271 pp.
A history including operations in the Gilberts, Marshalls, and Marianas. Sustained minor damage in the Battle of the Philippine Sea.

USS Chenango, CVE 28

927. The Chenangian, Victory Edition, 1942-1945. Los Angeles: Kater Engraving Co., 1945. 64 pp.
Pictorial history including operations at Tarawa, the Marshalls, and the Marianas.

USS Cowpens, CVL 25

928. The Story of the U.S.S. Cowpens (CVL-25). Baton Rouge: Army & Navy Pictorial Pubs., 1946. 49 pp.
Pictorial history including operations in the Marshalls, Marianas, and in the Battle of the Philippine sea.

USS Enterprise, CV 6

929. Ewing, Steve. USS Enterprise (CV-Six). The Most Decorated Ship of World War II. Missoula, MT: Pictorial Historical Pub. Co., 1982. 164 pp. DLC
Pictorial history of the ship's operations including the Central Pacific operations.

930. Saga of the U.S.S. Enterprise. New York: 1945. 8 lvs.
Very brief history of the ship.

931. Stafford, Edward P. The Big E. New York: Random House, 1962. 499 pp. DLC
Comprehensive history including operations at the Gilberts, Marshalls, and the Marianas.

932. U.S. Navy, USS Enterprise. "Narrative History and Chronological Order of Events, U.S.S. Enterprise (CV-6), 12 May 1938 - 25 September 1945." unpublished paper: Ships, 1 October 1945. 13 pp. DN
Brief wartime history of the carrier.

USS Essex, CV 9

933. Saga of the Essex. Baton Rouge: Army Navy Pub. Co., 1946. 141 pp. DN
Pictorial history including operations at Tarawa, Kwajalein, and with TF 58 at the Marianas.

NAVAL UNIT HISTORIES 115

934. Markey, Morris. <u>Well Done! An Aircraft Carrier in Battle Action</u>. New York: D. Appleton-Century Co., 1945. 223 pp. PCarlMH

USS Fanshaw Bay, CVE 70

935. <u>Straddled. A Short History of the U.S.S. Fanshaw Bay</u>. Seattle: Seattle Print. & Pub. Co., 1946. 72 pp.
Pictorial history including Saipan invasion, during which it sustained bomb damage.

USS Franklin, CV 13

936. <u>Big Ben, the Flat Top, the Story of the U.S.S. Franklin</u>. Atlanta: Albert Love Enterprises, ca1945. 68 lvs.
Pictorial history including its operations at Saipan.

USS Hoggatt Bay, CVE 75

937. <u>CVE-75, the Story of the U.S.S. Hoggatt Bay</u>. San Francisco: Newsfoto Pub. Co., 1946. 60 lvs.
Pictorial history including air support operations at Saipan.

USS Hornet, CV 12

938. <u>The United States Ship Hornet: First War Cruise, 1943-1945</u>. n.p.: 1945. 21 lvs. Mimeo NN
Brief history including supporting the operations at Majuro, the Marianas, and the Battle of the Philippine Sea. Ship's aircraft credited with sinking Japanese Carrier Hiji.

USS Intrepid, CV 11

939. Beach, Edward L. "The Fighting "I." <u>Warship International</u>, XVI, (Feb. 1979), pp. 157-161. DN
Pictorial review.

940. Roberts, John. <u>The Aircraft Carrier Intrepid</u>. Annapolis: Leeward Pubs., 1982. 96 pp.
Pictorial history with emphasis on the physical appearances and characteristics of the ship as well as the aircraft carried on board.

941. <u>The Saga of the U.S.S. Intrepid</u>. Los Angeles: Metropolitan Engravers, 1946. 168 pp.
Pictorial history including its operations in the Marshall Islands.

USS Langley, CVL 27

942. Monsarrat, John. Angel on the Yardarm. The Beginning of Fleet Radar Defense and the Kamikaze Threat. Newport, RI: Naval War College Press, 1985. 188 pp. DLC
Brief mention of Central Pacific operations.

USS Lexington, CV 16

943. Ewing, Steve. The "Lady Lex" and the "Blue Ghost." USS Lexington (CV-2 & CV 16). Missoula, MT: Pictorial Histories Pub. Co., 1983. 41 pp. DLC
Pictorial history of the two carriers that were named the Lexington. Strong emphasis on the physical characteristics of each ship.

944. Kinzey, Bert. USS Lexington in Scale and Detail. Blue Ridge Summit, PA: Tab Books, 1988. 72 pp. DLC
A detailed photographic history of the ship with emphasis on the physical characteristics.

945. Steichen, Edward. The Blue Ghost, a Photographic Log and Personal Narrative of the USS Lexington in Combat Operations. New York: Harcourt, Brace, 1947. 151 pp.
History of the ship's operations as told by its captain.

946. Tarawa to Tokyo... Los Angeles: 1945. 83 lvs.
Pictorial history including its operations at the Gilberts during which it sustained a torpedo hit.

USS Makassar Strait, CVE 91

947. The Mighty Mak (CVE-91). Seattle: Sterling Engraving Co., 1946. 36 lvs.
Pictorial history including operations at Kwajalein.

USS San Jacinto, CVL 54

948. A Short History of the U.S.S. San Jacinto, 3 May 1944 - 14 September 1945. San Francisco: Merrill Reed, 1945. 77 pp.
Pictorial history including operations in the Battle of the Philippine Sea and at Guam.

USS Saratoga, CV 3

949. Richards, Benjamin J., editor. Sara, the Story of the U.S.S. Saratoga. n.p.: 1945. 173 pp. DLC
Pictorial history including operations in the Gilberts and Marshalls.

USS Suwannee, CVE 27

950. War Log U.S.S. Suwannee CVE 27. Baton Rouge: Army & Navy Pictorial Pubs., 1946. 43 lvs.
Pictorial history including operations in the Gilberts, Marshalls, and the Marianas. Credited with sinking Japanese Submarine I-184 in the Battle of the Philippine Sea.

USS Wasp, CV 18

951. Prep Charlie: A History of the Peregrinations of Our Fighting Lady, USS Wasp while Mothering Air Group Eighty-one. New York: 1945. 206 pp.

952. Ferris, James S., editor, The Aircraft Carrier USS Wasp, CV-18. Boston: George E. Crosby, 1946. 105 pp.
Pictorial history including operations in the Marianas and the Battle of the Philippine Sea.

USS Yorktown, CV 10

953. Into the Wind. CV 10, USS Yorktown, World War II. n.p.: ca 1945. 160 pp.
Considered one of the best cruise books; a pictorial history including operations in the Marshalls and Marianas. Credited with damaging Japanese carrier Zuikaku in the Battle of the Philippine Sea.

954. Bryan, Joseph, III. Aircraft Carrier. New York: Ballantine Books, 1954. 205 pp. DLC

955. Friedman, Norman, and others, editors. USS Yorktown (CV10). Annapolis: Leeward Pubs., 1977. 52 pp. DLC
Pictorial history including line drawing of the ship with emphasis on the physical appearances and characteristics.

956. Reynolds, Clark G. The Fighting Lady: The "New Yorktown" in the Pacific War. Missoula, MT: Pictorial Historical Pub., 1986. 354 pp. DLC
Review of the carrier's operations with particular emphasis on the lives of the crew.

BATTLESHIPS

USS Alabama, BB 60

957. Lott, Arnold S., and Robert Summerall. USS Alabama (BB60). Pompton Lakes, NJ: Leeward Pubs., 1974. 36 pp. DLC
Pictorial history including line drawing of the ship with emphasis on the physical appearances and characteristics.

958. U.S. Navy, USS Alabama (BB-60), Aviation Unit. "History of Aviation Unit, USS Alabama, from Commissioning to 1 January 1945." unpublished paper: Ships, 1945. 19 pp. DN
Brief history of the spotting, scouting, etc. by the Ship's Aviation unit. Includes discussions of the Marshalls and Marianas operations.

959. War Diary, U.S.S. Alabama, 1942-1944. n.p.: 1945. 63 lvs. DN
Pictorial history including anti-aircraft support to the fast carrier task forces and as a fire support ship during the landing in the Gilberts, Marshalls, and Marianas.

USS California, BB 44

960. Smith, Myron J., Jr. Golden State Battlewagon. USS California (BB-44). Missoula, MT: Pictorial Histories Pub. Co., 1984. 44 pp. DLC
Pictorial history including line drawing of the ship with emphasis on the physical appearances and characteristics.

961. U.S. Navy, USS California (BB-44), Aviation Unit. "History of USS California, Aviation Unit." unpublished paper: Ships, 3 July 1945. 15 pp. DN
Review of the Aviation section operations, including a roster of personnel and summaries of flight times.

962. U.S.S. California: An Account of the Wartime Cruising of the USS California from Pearl Harbor to Tokyo Bay, 7 December 1941-3 October 1945. n.p.: 1946. 124 lvs.
Pictorial history including fire support at Saipan and Tinian.

USS Colorado, BB 45

963. The Colorado Cruise Book. Seattle: Litho by Craftman, 1946. 47 lvs.
Pictorial history including fire support at Tarawa and at Kwajalein, at which it received 22 hits from shore batteries, and in the Marianas.

USS Indiana, BB 58

964. 1945, U.S.S. Indiana. Berkeley: Lederer, Street & Zeus Co., 1945. 145 pp.
Pictorial history including fire support at Tarawa, the Marshalls and Marianas. Also with TF-58 in the Battle of the Philippine Sea.

965. U.S. Navy, USS Indiana (BB-58), Aviation Unit. "History of Aviation Unit, U.S.S. Indiana (BB-58)." unpublished paper: Ships, 1945. 14 pp. DN
Brief history from 30 April 1942 to 31 December 1944, with a supplement covering 1 Jan to 30 Mar 1945.

NAVAL UNIT HISTORIES   119

966. Smith, Myron J., Jr. The Sophisticated Lady, the Battleship Indiana in World War II. Fort Wayne: Fort Wayne Public Library, 1973. 51 pp. PCarlMH

967. War Diary, 1942-1945. n.p.: n.d. 158 pp.
Pictorial history.

IJN Kongo

968. Chihaya, Masataka, and Yasuo Abe. IJN Kongo/Battleship, 1912-1944. Winsdor, England, Profile Publications, 1971. pp. 265-268. DLC
Pictorial history with strong emphasis on physical characteristics; saw action in the Battle of the Philippine Sea.

USS Maryland, BB 46

969. U.S.S. Maryland, 1941-1945. Baton Rouge: Army Navy Pictorial Pub. Co., 1946. 47 pp.
Pictorial history including fire support at Tarawa, the Marshalls, and Marianas. Sustained a torpedo hit at Saipan.

970. Smith, Myron J., Jr. Free State Battlewagon. USS Maryland (BB-46). Missoula, MT: Pictorial Histories Pub. Co., 1986. 48 pp. DLC
Pictorial history including line drawing of the ship with emphasis on the physical appearances and characteristics.

USS Massachusetts, BB 59

971. Friedman, Norman, and others, editors. USS Massachusetts (BB 59). Annapolis: Leeward Pubs., 1979. 32 pp. DLC
Pictorial history including line drawing of the ship with emphasis on the physical appearances and characteristics.

972. A Pictorial History of the U.S.S. Massachusetts. San Antonio: Universal, 1945. 126 pp.
Pictorial history including operations in the Gilberts, Marshalls and the Marianas.

973. USS Massachusetts (BB59), Aviation Unit. "History of Aviation Unit, U.S.S. Massachusetts (BB-59)." unpublished paper: Ships, 1945. 95 pp. DN
Comprehensive history of the Aviation unit from May 1942 to July 1945, including review of the operations and personnel.

USS Mississippi, BB 41

974. U.S.S. Mississippi War Record, 1941-1945. Baltimore: Thomsen-Ellis-Hutton Co., 1945. 126 pp.
Pictorial history including operations at Tarawa and in the Marshalls.

USS New Jersey, BB 62

975. War Log, U.S.S New Jersey, 1943-1945. St. Louis: 1946. 95 pp.
Pictorial history of operations including the Marshalls, Marianas, and the Battle of the Philippine Sea.

USS North Carolina, BB 55

976. The Showboat, BB 55, USS North Carolina. n.p.: ca1946. 71 lvs.
Pictorial history including operations at Tarawa, and in the Marshalls and Marianas.

977. Lott, Arnold S., and Robert F. Summerall, editors. USS North Carolina (BB55). Pompton Lakes, NJ: Leeward Pubs., 1973. 32 pp. DLC
Pictorial history with emphasis on the physical characteristics and appearances.

978. USS North Carolina (BB-55), Aviation Unit. "History of Aviation Unit, U.S.S. North Carolina (BB-55)." unpublished paper: Ships, 1945. 3 pp. DN
Very brief history of the unit from May 1941 through May 1944.

USS Pennsylvania, BB 38

979. Cates, Clifton B. War History of the U.S.S. Pennsylvania BB (38). Seattle: Metropolitan Press, 1946. 65 pp.
Pictorial history including fire support at Makin, the Marshalls, and the Marianas.

980. Smith, Myron J., Jr. Keystone Battlewagon. U.S.S. Pennsylvania, (BB-38). Charleston, WV: Pictorial Histories Pub. Co., 1983. 44 pp. DLC
Pictorial history including line drawing of the ship with emphasis on the physical appearances and characteristics.

USS South Dakota, BB 57

981. U.S.S. South Dakota. Washington: Government Printing Office, 1950. 11 pp. PCarlMH
Brief history of operations.

982. U.S.S. South Dakota, Aviation Unit. "History of Aviation Unit, U.S.S. South Dakota (BB-57)." unpublished paper: Ships, 1945. 8 pp. DN
Brief history of the unit from May 2, 1942 to April 1, 1945.

USS Tennessee, BB 43

983. USS Tennessee, December 7, 1941 - December 7, 1945.
Philadelphia: Clark Print. House, 1946. 209 pp.
Pictorial history including fire support operations at Tarawa and in the Marshalls and the Marianas.

984. Warship Profile No. 21: U.S.S. Tennessee. Windsor, England: Profile Pubs., 1972. pp. 197-200.
Brief pictorial history with emphasis on the physical characteristics and appearances.

USS Washington, BB 56

985. Baker, R. W., editor. History of the USS Washington, 1941-1945. New York: R. W. Kelly Pub. Corp., 1946. 116 pp.
Pictorial history including operations at Tarawa, the Marshalls, Marianas, and in the Battle of the Philippine Sea.

986. Musicant, Ivan. Battleship at War. The Story of the USS Washington. New York: Harcourt Brace Jovanovich Pubs., 1986. 364 pp. DLC
Comprehensive history of the ship and its operations.

CRUISERS

USS Baltimore, CA 68

987. The History of the U.S.S. Baltimore CA-68. San Angelo, TX: Newsfoto Pub. Co., 1946. 117 lvs.
Pictorial history including fire support at the invasions of the Marshall and Marianas Islands. Also participated in the Battle of the Philippine Sea.

USS Biloxi, CL 80

988. U.S.S. Biloxi (CL 80). San Francisco: Schwabacher-Frey Co., ca1945. 44 lvs.
Pictorial history of operations including the screening of the fast carrier groups and the bombardment of Marshalls and Marianas Islands.

USS Birmingham, CL 62

989. The Saga of the U.S.S. Birmingham: The Compilation of Her Officers and Men. San Angelo, TX: Newsfoto Pub. Co., 1946. 96 lvs.
Pictorial history including operations in the Marianas and the Battle of the Philippine Sea.

122   THE CENTRAL PACIFIC CAMPAIGN, 1943-1944

USS Boston, CA 69

990. U.S.S. Boston CA-69. San Angelo, TX: Newsfoto Pub. Co., 1946. 64 lvs.
Pictorial history including operations in the Marshalls and Marianas, and in the Battle of the Philippine Sea.

USS Cleveland, CL 55

991. United States Ship Cleveland... Andover, MA: Andover Press, 1946. 79 pp.
Pictorial history including its operations in the Marianas.

USS Denver, CL 58

992. Life Aboard the U.S.S. Denver, a Biography of the CL 58, 1942-1945. Baltimore: Thomsen-Ellis-Hutton Co., 1946. 39 pp.
Pictorial history including its operations in the Marianas.

USS Louisville, CA 28

993. Man of War, Log of the United States Heavy Cruiser Louisville... Philadelphia: Dunlap Print. Co., 1946. 212 pp.
Pictorial history including fire support operations at the Marshalls and Marianas.

USS Miami, CL 89

994. The Story of United States Ship Miami (CL 89) in Words and Pictures. Baton Rouge: Army & Navy Pictorial Pub. Co., 1946. 47 pp.
Pictorial history including operations in the Marianas.

USS Minneapolis, CA 36

995. Luey, Allen T., and H. P. Bruvold. The "Minnie," or the War Cruise of the U.S.S. Minneapolis. Elkhart, IN: Bell Print. Co., 1946. 126 pp.
Pictorial history including operations at Tarawa, the Marshalls, and the Battle of the Philippine Sea.

996. USS Minneapolis (CA-36), Aviation Unit. "History of Aviation Unit, VCS-6, U.S.S. Minneapolis (CA-36)." unpublished paper: Ships, 1945. 4 pp. DN
Brief history from Jan. 1944-Apr. 1945, and July-Aug. 1945.

NAVAL UNIT HISTORIES   123

USS Mobile, CL 63

997. The Story of a Ship, USS Mobile and the Men Who Fought Her. Long Beach, CA: Greens, 1945. 80 lvs.
Pictorial history including operations in the Gilberts, Marshalls, and the Marianas.

USS Montpelier, CL 57

998. Fahey, James J. Pacific War Diary. Boston: Houghton Mifflin Co., 1963. 404 pp. DLC
Author was a seaman providing insight into the day to day activities aboard a cruiser.

999. War Diary of CL 57, U.S.S. Montpelier, September 1942-December 1945... New York: Robert W. Kelly Pub. Corp., 1945. 39 lvs.
Pictorial history including operations at Saipan and in the Battle of the Philippine Sea.

USS New Orleans, CA 32

1000. Forgy, Howell M. "...and Pass the Ammunition." New York: 1944. 242 pp.
Author was chaplain; of limited usefulness due to wartime censorship.

1001. Carters, Clyde, Jr. The No Boat: The Unfinished Story of the U.S.S. New Orleans. Berkeley, CA: James J. Gillick & Co., 1945. 14 lvs.
Brief pictorial history including operations at Tarawa and in the Marshalls and Marianas.

1002. USS New Orleans (CA-32), Aviation Unit. "History of the Aviation Unit, U.S.S. New Orleans (CA-32)." unpublished paper: Ships, 1945. 25 pp. DN
Review of activities including a chronology of operations from 7 December 1941 thru 31 December 1944.

USS Pensacola, CA 24

1003. A History of the U.S.S. Pensacola, With Emphasis on the Years She Served in the Pacific Against the Japanese During World War II. San Francisco: Philips and Van Orden, 1946. 108 pp.
Pictorial history of operations including Tarawa and the Marshalls.

1004. U.S.S. Pensacola, (CA-24), Aviation Unit. "History of Aviation Unit, U.S.S. Pensacola (CA-24)." unpublished paper: Ships, 1945. 8 pp. DN
Brief history of operations.

124   THE CENTRAL PACIFIC CAMPAIGN, 1943-1944

USS Portland, CA 33

1005. USS Portland (CA-33), Aviation Unit. "History of Aviation Unit, U.S.S. Portland (CA-33)." unpublished paper: Ships, 1 July 1945. 7 pp. DN
Brief history including its operations at Tarawa.

USS St. Louis, CL 49

1006. USS St. Louis (CL-49), Aviation Unit. "History of Aviation Unit, U.S.S. St. Louis (CL-49)." unpublished paper: Ships, 1945. 29 pp. DN
Brief history including its service at Guam.

USS Salt Lake City, CA 25

1007. The Story of the U.S.S. Salt Lake City, 1929 to 1946. Long Beach, CA: Greens´s, 1946. 72 pp.
Pictorial history including operations in the Gilberts and Marshalls.

USS San Diego, CL 53

1008. U.S.S San Diego in World War II. n.p.: n.d.
Pictorial history including operations in the Gilberts, Marshalls, and with the Fast Carriers in the Battle of the Philippine Sea.

USS San Francisco, CA 38

1009. One Ship, U.S.S. San Francisco, the Crew´s Cruise Book. San Francisco: Crocker Union Litho. Co., 1945. 41 lvs.
Pictorial history including operations at Tarawa and in the Marshalls.

1010. U.S. Navy, USS San Francisco (CL-38), Aviation Unit. "History of Aviation Unit, U.S.S. San Francisco, (CA-38)." unpublished paper: Ships, 27 Aug 1945. 32 pp. DN
Brief history including operations in the Gilberts, Kwajalein, and the Marianas.

USS San Juan, CL 54

1011. Hines, E. G. Panther Strikes, a History of the U.S.S. San Juan CL 54. Seattle: Sterling Engraving, 1945.
Pictorial history including operations in the Gilberts, Marshalls, Marianas, and in the Battle of the Philippine Sea.

NAVAL UNIT HISTORIES   125

USS Sante Fe, CL 60

1012. <u>USS Sante Fe Cruise Record</u>. Chicago: Rogers Print. Co., 1946. 169 pp.
Pictorial history including operations in the Gilberts, Marshalls, Marianas, and the Battle of the Philippine Sea.

1013. U.S. Navy, USS Sante Fe (CL-60), Aviation Unit. "History of Aviation Unit, U.S.S. Sante Fe (CL-60)." unpublished paper: Ships, 5 April 1945. 6 pp. DN
Brief history including operations in the Gilberts, Marshalls, and Marianas.

USS Vincennes, CL 64

1014. Dorris, Donald H. <u>A Log of the Vincennes</u>. Louisville: Standard Print. Co., 1947. 402 pp.
Pictorial history including operations with the Fast Carriers in the Marianas.

1015. U.S. Navy, U.S.S. Vincennes (CL-64), Aviation Unit. "History of Aviation Unit, U.S.S. Vincennes (CL-64)." unpublished paper: Ships, July 1945. 11 pp. DN
Brief history including operations in the Marianas.

USS Wichita, CA 45

1016. <u>300,000 Miles to Victory</u>. n.p.: ca1945. 86 pp.
Pictorial history including operations in the Marshalls and Marianas, and in the Battle of the Philippine Sea.

DESTROYERS

USS Anthony, DD 515

1017. <u>The Mad Anthony, the Story of a Ship and Her Men</u>. Charleston, SC: Southern Print. & Pub. Co., 1946. 24 pp.
Pictorial history including its operations as fire support ship in the invasions of the Marianas Islands. Also rescued several pilots whose planes had run out of gas and had ditched.

USS Bennion, DD 662

1018. <u>The Story of the Bennion</u>. n.p.: 1946. 110 pp.
Pictorial history including operations as a fighter director and radar picket ship during the Marianas operations.

USS Cassin Young, DD 793

1019. Harmon, J. Scott. <u>USS Cassin Young, DD-793, a Fletcher Class Destroyer</u>. Missoula, MT: Pictorial Historical Pub. Co., ca1985. 48 pp. DLC
Pictorial history including line drawing of the ship with emphasis on the physical appearances and characteristics.

USS Heywood L. Edwards, DD 663

1020. <u>War Diary of the U.S.S. H. L. Edwards</u>. Seattle: Sterling Engraving Co., 1945. 20 lvs.
Brief history including fire support operations at Saipan and Tinian.

USS Meade, DD 602

1021. Greenspan, Harry. <u>The Album of U.S.S. Meade</u>. n.p.: 1945. 72 lvs.
History of operations including fire support at Tarawa and the Marshalls.

USS Ringgold, DD 500

1022. <u>The Officers and Men of the U.S.S Ringgold Bid You a Cordial Welcome...at Sea, October 1945</u>. n.p.: 1945. 14 pp.
Brief history including close fire support operations at Tarawa, the Marshalls, and the Marianas.

USS Saufley, DD 465

1023. <u>U.S.S. Saufley (DD 465), Her Story</u>. Charleston: Walker, Evans & Cogswell Co., 1946. 54 pp.
Pictorial history including operations as a fire support ship at Saipan and Tinian.

IJN Yukikaze

1024. Chihaya, Masataka, and Yasuo Abe. <u>Warship Profile 22, IJN Yukikaze/Destroyer, 1939-1970</u>. Windsor, Berkshire: Profile Pubs., 1972. 221-244 pp. DLC
Pictorial history with emphasis on physical characteristics.

NAVAL UNIT HISTORIES 127

DESTROYER ESCORTS

USS Abercrombie, DE 373

1025. Stafford, Edward P. Little Sky, Big War. The Saga of DE 373. New York: William Morrow & Co., 1984. 336 pp. DLC
Saw action in the Battle of the Philippine Sea.

SUBMARINES

USS Halibut, SS 232

1026. Galantin, I. J. Take Her Deep. A Submarine Against Japan in World War II. Chapel Hill, NC: Algonquin Books, 1987. 262 pp. DLC
Written by commanding officer; includes a patrol in the Marianas Islands area.

USS Silversides, SS 236

1027. Trumbull, Robert. Silversides. New York: Henry Holt and Co., 1945. 217 pp. DLC
Credited with sinking six Japanese ships during a patrol in the Marianas Islands area.

TRANSPORTS

USS Alcyone, AKA 7

1028. The Saga of an AKA. Philadelphia: Campus Pub. Co., 1945. 32 lvs.
Pictorial history including the invasion of the Gilberts, Kwajalein, and Saipan.

USS Comet, AP 166

1029. Following the Comet's Tale. San Francisco: Schwabacher-Frey Co., 1946. 93 pp.
Pictorial history including the invasion of Saipan.

USS Custer, APA 40

1030. U.S.S. Custer. n.p.: 1945. 16 lvs.
Brief pictorial history including the Marshall Islands operations.

USS Doyen, APA 1

1031. Marsden, Lawrence A. Attack Transport. The Story of the U.S.S. Doyen. Minneapolis: Univ. of Minnesota Press, 1945. 200 pp.
Participated in the Marshalls and Marianas operations.

USS Harry Lee, APA 10

1032. History of the U.S.S. Harry Lee, 1940-1945... n.p.: 1945. 12 lvs.
Brief history including operations at Kwajalein and Guam.

USS Herald of the Morning, AP 173

1033. [Cruise book of the U.S.S. Herald of the Morning, 1944-1946]. Seattle: Sterling Engraving Co., 1946. 18 lvs.
Brief history including the invasion of Saipan.

NAVAL CONSTRUCTION UNITS

4th Naval Construction Battalion

1036. Lil' Short Runner Presents the Fourth U.S. Naval Construction Battalion Penguin, 1944-45. Baton Rouge: Army Navy Pub. Co., 1945. 171 pp.   DLC
Pictorial history including service on Guam.

7th Naval Construction Battalion

1037. Redditt, James H. The Log, a Battalion Picture Biography. Baton Rouge: Army Navy Pub. Co., 1945. 66 lvs.
Pictorial history of operations including service on Saipan.

13th Naval Construction Battalion

1038. Pictorial Record of the 13th Naval Construction Battalion, 1942-1943. n.p.: ca1943. 18 lvs.   NN
Pictorial history of unit which later participated in the capture and occupation of Guam.

1039. 13th U.S.N.C.B. Second Cruise. n.p.: 13th Naval Construction Bn., 1946. 200 pp.
Pictorial history including participation in the capture and occupation of Guam.

NAVAL UNIT HISTORIES   129

16th Naval Construction Battalion

1040. <u>16th Naval Construction Battalion Yearbook.</u> n.p.: 1945. 84 lvs.
Pictorial history including participation in the Gilbert Islands operations.

18th Naval Construction Battalion

1041. <u>Cruise Book, Eighteenth Special Naval Construction Battalion.</u> n.p.: 1945. 29 lvs. NN
Pictorial history including participation in the capture and occupation of Tinian.

1042. <u>The Odyssey, Eighteenth U.S. Naval Construction Battalion.</u> San Francisco: 1946. 94 pp. DLC
Comprehensive pictorial history including the capture and occupation of Tinian.

20th Special Naval Construction Battalion

1043. <u>Log of the 20th Battalion, 1st Cruise, 1942-1944.</u> Baton Rouge: Army & Navy Pub. Co., 1945. 99 pp.
Pictorial history including service on Saipan.

21st Naval Construction Battalion

1044. <u>The Blackjack, 1944-1945. A Story About and Published by the 21st U.S. Naval Construction Battalion.</u> Baton Rouge: Army Navy Pub. Co., 1946. 190 pp. DLC
Pictorial history including service on Saipan.

1045. <u>21st U.S. Naval Construction Battalion, 1942-1943: Souvenir Annual.</u> n.p.: ca1944. 18 lvs.
Pictorial review of early operations.

27th Naval Construction Battalion

1046. Donahue, Ralph J. <u>Ready on the Right, a True Story of a Naturalist-Seabee on the Islands of Kodiak, Unalaska, Adak, Tanaga, Oahu, Eniwetok, Guam, MogMog (Ulithi), and Okinawa.</u> Kansas City, MO: Smith Print. Co., 1946. 194 [19] pp.
Pictorial history of operations.

1047. Triest, Willard G. <u>Danger, Fighting Men At Work. A Work-a-day Tale of How the Job Was Actually Done by the 27th Seabees...</u> Baton Rouge: Army & Navy Pictorial Pub. Co., 1945. 196 pp.
Pictorial review.

130 THE CENTRAL PACIFIC CAMPAIGN, 1943-1944

36th Naval Construction Battalion

1048. <u>36th Naval Construction Battalion, January 1945</u>. Baton Rouge: Army & Navy Pub. Co., 1945. 56 pp.
Pictorial history including service on Saipan.

38th Naval Construction Battalion

1049. Herman, W. A., and others, editors. <u>2nd Saga of the 38 NCB. Aleutians, Adak, Kodiak, Kiska; Oahu; Marianas; Japan, Sasebo, Kure, Yokosuka</u>. n.p.: ca1946. 135 pp.
Pictorial history including service on Tinian.

1050. Brooks, R. M., and others, editors. <u>The 38th N.C.B. Saga</u>... San Francisco: A. Carlisle & Co., ca1944. 160 pp. NN
Pictorial history including service on Tinian.

48th Naval Construction Battalion

1051. Turner, Jack W., editor. <u>Tradewinds. Souvenir Edition</u>. n.p.: ca1945. [64] pp. MiU
Pictorial history including participation in the capture and occupation of Guam.

52nd Naval Construction Battalion

1052. <u>Yearbook, 1942-1944,</u>... St. Louis: 1944. 132 pp. NN
Pictorial history including service on Guam.

53rd Naval Construction Battalion

1053. <u>History of the 53rd N.C.B., February 1943 to February 1946</u>. Baton Rouge: Army Navy Pub. Co., 1946. 121 pp.
Pictorial history including participation in the capture and occupation of Guam.

1054. U.S. Navy, Construction Battalion 53. "United States Naval Construction Battalion 53." unpublished paper: Shore Establishments, n.d. 10 pp. DN
Brief history of activities, including participation in the invasion of Guam.

67th Naval Construction Battalion

1055. <u>Pictorial Log, 67th Naval Construction Battalion</u>. Baton Rouge: Army Navy Pub. Co., 1945. 101 pp. NN
Pictorial history including service on Tinian.

NAVAL UNIT HISTORIES 131

70th Naval Construction Battalion

1056. <u>USN 70th Construction Battalion</u>. Baton Rouge: Army Navy Pub. Co., ca1945. 2 vols.
Pictorial history including service on Guam.

74th Naval Construction Battalion

1057. <u>74th Battalion in Review, 1943-1944</u>. Berkeley: Lederer, Street & Zeus, Inc., 1945. 158 pp.
Pictorial history including operations in the Gilberts.

1058. U.S. Navy, Construction Battalion 74. "United States Naval Construction Battalion 74." unpublished paper: Shore Establishments, n.d. 5 pp. DN
Brief history of operations including those on Tarawa.

87th Naval Construction Battalion

1059. <u>The Earthmover: A Chronicle of the 87th Seabee Battalion in World War II</u>. Baton Rouge: Army & Navy Pub. Co., 1946. 368 pp. NN
Pictorial history including service on Saipan.

92nd Naval Construction Battalion

1060. <u>Log. Tinian, Marshall Islands</u>. n.p.: n.d. DLC

1061. Streibig, K. C., editor. <u>The Ninety-second Naval Construction Battalion Log for the Year Ending...May, Nineteen Hundred and Forty-four - [Nineteen Hundred and Forty-five]</u>. Honolulu: ca1945. 129, 8 pp. NN
Pictorial history of operations.

95th Naval Construction Battalion

1062. <u>The Cruise Record April 1943-September 1945, a Record of Achievement</u>. Chicago: Rogers Print. Co., ca1945. NN
Pictorial history including operations in the Gilbert Islands.

100th Naval Construction Battalion

1063. <u>Pictorial Review, U.S. Naval Construction Battalion Number 100...</u> Harrisburg: J. H. McFarland Co., 1945. 2 vols. NN
Pictorial history including operations in the Marshall Islands.

101st Naval Construction Battalion

1064. Peterson, A. J., and John Newall, Jr., editors. "A Stone's Throw From Tokyo." A Pictorial Overseas History of the 101st Seabees. n.p.: 1945. NN
Pictorial history including service on Saipan.

103rd Naval Construction Battalion

1065. Tour of Duty, 103 Naval Construction Battalion, 1943-1945. Baton Rouge: Army & Navy Pub. Co., 1946. 177 pp.
Pictorial history including service on Guam.

105th Naval Construction Battalion

1066. 105 Naval Construction Battalion. San Francisco: Crocker Union Co., 1945. 76 lvs. DLC
Pictorial history including service on Kwajalein.

107th Naval Construction Battalion

1067. The Log, 1943-1945: A Story of the Seabee Battalion Conceived in War, Dedicated to Peace. Baton Rouge: Army & Navy Pub. Co., 1946. 208 pp. DLC
Pictorial history including service on Kwajalein and Tinian.

109th Naval Construction Battalion

1068. 1943-1944, CIX Annual. n.p.: 1945. 129 pp.
Pictorial history including service on Roi-Namur and Guam.

110th Naval Construction Battalion

1069. "Contract Completed". Baton Rouge: Army & Navy Pub. Co., 1946. 85 lvs. NN
Pictorial history including service on Eniwetok and Tinian.

117th Naval Construction Battalion

1070. The Bulldog Travels. n.p.: ca1945. 204 pp.
Pictorial history including service on Saipan.

1071. The 117th Review, Anniversary Edition. Honolulu: Paradise of the Pacific, Ltd., 1945. 55 pp.
Pictorial history including service on Saipan.

NAVAL UNIT HISTORIES 133

121st Naval Construction Battalion

1072. McKerracher, Mac, and others, editors. Battalion History, May 10, 1943-August 15, 1945. Baton Rouge: Army & Navy Pictorial Pubs., 1946. 91 pp. DLC
Pictorial history including service on Roi-Namur, Kwajalein, Saipan and Tinian.

128th Naval Construction Battalion

1073. One Twenty Eighth U.S.N. Construction Battalion (Pontoon), 1944-1945. Pacific Offensive... Chicago: 1946. 99 pp.
Pictorial history including service on Guam.

135th Naval Construction Battalion

1074. Organ, F. P., editor. The 135th U.S. Naval Construction Battalion Review. n.p.: 1946. DLC
Pictorial history including service on Tinian.

136th Naval Construction Battalion

1075. Photo Memories of a Seabee Battalion. Yokosuka, Japan: 1945. DLC
Pictorial history including service on Guam.

141st Naval Construction Battalion

1076. Souvenir Muster Book 141st U.S. Navy Construction Battalion, Sept. 1944. n.p.: 96 pp.
Pictorial history including service on Kwajalein.

301st Naval Construction Battalion

1077. 301st U.S. Naval Construction Battalion, April 1944 to December 1945. n.p.: n.d. 247 pp. NN
Pictorial history of harbor construction activities on Roi-Namur, Kwajalein, Saipan, and Guam.

302nd Naval Construction Battalion

1078. 302 Naval Construction Battalion, a Picture Story of Our Part in Eight Major Invasions. San Francisco: Crocker Union, 1945. 106 lvs.
Pictorial history including participation in the capture and occupation of Guam.

NAVAL AIR UNITS

AIR GROUPS

Air Group 3

1079. *Air Group 3.* n.p.: 1945. 14 pp.
Brief history of the group aboard the Yorktown, CV 10.

Air Group 7

1080. Barton, R. S., and R. G. Hanecak, editors. *Air Group Seven.*
n.p.: ca1945. 132 pp. Photos. NN
Pictorial history of the group aboard the Bon Homme Richard, CV 31

Air Group 9

1081. *Air Group 9 Second Pacific Cruise, March 1944-July 1945, U.S.S. Lexington and U.S.S. Yorktown.* Allentown, PA: Miers-Bachman, 1945. 88 pp.
Pictorial history including service in the Gilbert, Marshall and Marianas Islands.

1082. *U.S.S. Essex, Carrier Air Group 9. The Record of the First Two Years, From the Forming of the Air Group in March 1942 To the Return From Action Against the Enemy in March 1944.* Chicago: Lakeside Press, 1945. 119 pp.
Pictorial history including operations in the Gilberts.

Air Group 15

1083. Hoyt, Edwin P. *McCampbell's Heroes. The Story of the U.S. Navy's Celebrated Carrier Fights in the Pacific War.* New Van Nostrand, Reinhold Co., 1983. 272 pp. DLC
Served on Hornet CV-12; includes operations in the Marianas.

Air Group 16

1084. Bryan, Joseph, III, and Philip Reed. *Mission Beyond Darkness.* New York: Duell, Sloan and Pierce, 1945. 133 pp. DLC
Account of operations in the Battle of the Philippine Sea, June 1944.

NAVAL UNIT HISTORIES   135

Air Group 20

1085. Air Group 20, an Unofficial Portrayal of Carrier Air Group Twenty U.S. Pacific Fleet From Commissioning To Completion of Combat Cruise, 1943-1945: Compiled From Private and Naval Sources in 1949. n.p.: 1949. 84 pp.
Pictorial history of group on board the Lexington, CV-16, including service in the Marshalls and Marianas.

Air Group 60

1086. Peyton, Green. 5,000 Miles Toward Tokyo. Norman, OK: Univ. of Oklahoma Press, 1945. 173 pp.   DLC
Personal narrative by an airman who served with the group on the Suwannee CVE-27 in the Marshalls and Marianas.

86th Air Group

1087. Camp, Robert, Jr., editor. Carrier Air Group 86. n.p.: 1946. 280 pp.
Group served on Wasp, CV-18.

SQUADRONS

Fighter Squadron 2

1088. Morrissey, Thomas L. Odyssey of Fighting Two. Philadelphia: Lyon & Armor, 1945. 207 pp.
Author was Air Combat Intelligence Officer in the squadron on board the Enterprise, CV-6 and Hornet, CV-12.

Photographic Interpretation Squadron 2

1089. Interpron Two, the Record of Our Squadron, How We Worked, Lived, and Played. n.p.: 1945. 140 pp.
Pictorial history including its service on Guam.

Fighting Squadron 10

1090. Mersky, Peter. The Grim Reapers, Fighting Squadron Ten in WWII. Mesa, AZ: Champlin Museum Press, 1986. 131 pp.   DLC
Group served on Enterprise, CV-6 throughout the Central Pacific campaign.

136   THE CENTRAL PACIFIC CAMPAIGN, 1943-1944

Fighting Squadron 16

1091. Anderson, Robert E., editor. Was this Pastel? n.p.: 1947. 16 pp.
Served on Lexington, CV-16; includes operations in the Gilberts and Marshalls.

Bombing Squadron 17

1092. Gault, Owen. "How Bombing 17 Tamed the Beast." Air Classics, VIII (Apr 1972), pp. 10-15. DLC
Review of problems encountered by a unit using the Curtiss SC-2 Helldiver for the first time.

1093. Olds, Robert. Helldiver Squadron, the Story of Carrier Bombing Squadron 17, with Task Force 58. New York: Dodd, Mead, 1944. 255 pp. DLC
Eyewitness account of the early deployment of the SCB "Helldiver" with BS-17 thru February 1944.

Torpedo Squadron 17

1094. Torpedo Squadron 17. San Francisco: James H. Barry, 1945. 67 pp.
Served on Bunker Hill, CV-17, with Task Force 58.

Fighting Squadron 23

1095. U.S. Navy, Pacific Fleet and Pacific Ocean Area, Fighting Squadron 23. "Story of Fighting 23." unpublished paper: Type Command File, 1963. 67 pp. DN
Brief chronology of unit from November 16, 1942 to May 11, 1944.

Fighting Squadron 31

1096. Winston, Robert A. Fighting Squadron: A Veteran Squadron Leader's First-hand Account of Carrier Combat with Task Force 58. New York: Holliday House, 1946. 182 pp.
Unit served aboard Cabot, CVL-28 and Belleau Woods, CVL-24.

Fighting Squadron 46

1097. Ziesing, Hibben. History of Fighting Squadron 46: A Log in Narrative Form of Its Participation in World War II. New York: Plantin Press, 1946. 43 pp.
Served on USS Independence, CVL 22; pioneered night carrier operations off Eniwetok.

Bombing Squadron 109

1098. Miller, Norman M. *I Took the Sky Road.* New York: Dodd, Mead, 1945. 212 pp. DLC
Personal narrative by a pilot who served with the squadron.

1099. Steele, Theodore M. *A Pictorial Record of the Combat Duty of Bombing Squadron 109 in the Central Pacific, 28 December 1943 - 14 August 1944.* n.p.: 1944.
Includes operations in the Marshalls.

MISCELLANEOUS AVIATION UNITS

NAVAL AIR TRANSPORT SERVICE

1100. Lee, James. *Operation Lifeline, History and Development of the Naval Air Transport Service.* Chicago: Ziff Davis Pub. Co., 1947. 171 pp. DN
Pictorial history of the development and operations of the Naval Air Transport Service.

MISCELLANEOUS UNITS

Mobile Explosives Investigations Unit 4

1101. Mobile Explosives Investigations Unit 4. "History of Mobile Explosives Investigations Unit 4." unpublished paper: Shore Establishments, 5 Sept 1945. 7 pp. DN
Brief history including its operations on Tarawa, Guam, and Saipan.

Amphibious Group 5

1102. U.S. Navy, Pacific Fleet and Pacific Ocean Area. "The History of Amphibious Group Five, June 1944 to August 1945." unpublished paper: Type Commands, n.d. 70 pp. DN
Chronological narrative of operations including Guam and Saipan.

Transport Squadron 11

1103. U.S. Navy, Transport Squadron 11. "Transport Squadron Eleven, including Transport Divisions Twenty and Twenty One." unpublished paper: Type Commands, n.d. 9 pp. DN
Brief history of operations, including the invasions of Makin Atoll, Eniwetok, Saipan, and Guam.

138   THE CENTRAL PACIFIC CAMPAIGN, 1943-1944

Transport Squadron Twelve Command

1104. Scott, Walter H. "A Brief History of Transport Squadron Twelve Command." unpublished paper: Individual Personnel, 1945. 87 pp. DN
Account of the landings at Saipan and Guam, as well as other operations. Biographical sketches of officers and enlisted personnel are included.

Landing Ship Tank Flotilla 13

1105. "War History of the LST Flotilla Thirteen." unpublished paper: Type Commands, 1945. 20 pp. DN
History of operations including a chronology and roster. Saw service in the Gilbert, Marshall, and Marianas invasions.

Transport Squadron 14

1106. U.S. Navy, Transport Squadron 14. "Command History of Transport Squadron Fourteen, United States Fleet, 3 September 1943 to 14 August 1945." unpublished paper: Type Commands, n.d. 36 pp. DN
History of its operations, including the invasions of Saipan and Tinian.

Transport Squadron 20

1107. U.S. Navy, Transport Squadron 20. "Transport Squadron Twenty." unpublished paper: Type Commands, n.d. 18 pp. DN
Brief history and chronology of its operations, including Eniwetok.

Transport Squadron 21

1108. U.S. Navy, Transport Squadron 21. "Transport Squadron Twenty-one." unpublished paper: Type Commands, n.d. 5 pp. DN
Brief history of operations during 1945 including Eniwetok.

Landing Ship Tank Flotilla 31

1109. "War History of the LST Flotilla Thirty-one." unpublished paper: Type Commands, 1946. 4 pp. DN
History of operations including service in the Marianas invasion.

Landing Ship Tank Flotilla 32

1110. "War History of the LST Flotilla Thirty-two." unpublished paper: Type Commands, 1945. 12 pp. DN
History of operations including in the Marshalls and Marianas areas.

NAVAL UNIT HISTORIES   139

Landing Ship Tank Flotilla 34

1111. "War History of the LST Flotilla Thirty-four." unpublished paper: Type Commands, 1945. 12 pp. DN
History of preparations including service in the Marshalls and Marianas areas.

Task Force 58

1112. Busch, Noel F. "Task Force 58". Life, XVII (July 17, 1944), pp. 17-25. DLC
Pictorial account of operations during the Marianas campaign.

1113. Jensen, Oliver O. "Carrier War: The Story of Mighty Task Force 58." Life, XVIII (Mar 26, 1945), pp. 77-88. DLC
Pictorial review of operations.

Task Force Group 96.1

1114. U.S. Navy, Task Group 96.1, Shore-Based Air Force, Marshalls-Gilberts Area. "Command History." unpublished paper: Admin. Hist. Appen. 18E, 30 Aug 1945. 97 pp. DN
History of the Naval and Marine Aviation units assigned to area during the war, including VMSB-331, VMB-613, VMF-111, VS-66, and VPB-144.

Task Force Group 96.3

1115. Marshalls - Gilbert Patrol and Escort Group. "Wartime History of Task Force Group 96.3." unpublished paper: Admin. Hist. Appen. 18 (E), 28 Aug 1945. 7 pp. DN
Brief history of the convoy protection activities between the Marshalls and forward area ports.

Transport Division 105

1116. U.S. Navy, Transport Division 105. "History of Transport Division One Hundred Five." unpublished paper: Type Commands, n.d. 9 pp. DN
Brief history of operations during 1945, including those on Guam.

UNDERWATER DEMOLITION TEAMS

Demolition Teams 1 & 2

1117. U.S. Navy, Underwater Demolition Teams 1 & 2. "History of Underwater Demolition Teams 1 & 2." unpublished paper: Shore Establishments, 1947. 7 pp. DN
Brief account of operations on Tarawa and the Marshalls.

Demolition Team 3

1118. U.S. Navy, Underwater Demolition Team 3. "History of Underwater Demolition Team 3." unpublished paper: Shore Establishments, 1945. 15 pp. DN
Brief account of operations including the Marianas, and a roster of personnel.

Demolition Team 4

1119. U.S. Navy, Underwater Demolition Team 4. "History of Underwater Demolition Team 4." unpublished paper: Shore Establishments, n.d. 6 pp. DN
Brief account of operations, including Guam, and a roster of personnel.

Demolition Team 5

1120. U.S. Navy, Underwater Demolition Team 5. "History of Underwater Demolition Team 5." unpublished paper: Shore Establishments, n.d. 18 pp. DN
Brief account of operations, including the Marianas, and a roster of personnel.

Demolition Team 6

1121. U.S. Navy, Underwater Demolition Team 6. "History of Underwater Demolition Team 6." unpublished paper: Shore Establishments, n.d. 4 pp. DN
Very brief account of operations, including the Marianas, and a roster of personnel.

Demolition Team 7

1122. U.S. Navy, Underwater Demolition Team 7. "History of Underwater Demolition Team 7." unpublished paper: Shore Establishments, n.d. 16 pp. DN
Brief account of operations, including the Marianas, and a roster of personnel.

NAVAL UNIT HISTORIES

BASES AND SHORE INSTALLATIONS

Mine Assembly Depot No. 4

1123. U.S. Navy, Tinian, Marianas, Mine Assembly Depot No. 4. "Administrative History and Phase Analysis of Mine Assembly Depot Number 4." unpublished paper: Shore Establishments, 11 Aug 1945. 12 pp. DN
Brief history of the depot activities including graphs indicating mine production for 1945.

Naval Operating Base No. 6

1124. Hammer, David H. Lion Six. Annapolis: U.S. Naval Institute Press, 1947. 107 pp. DLC
History of Naval Operating Base on Guam.

1125. _____ _____ United States Naval Institute Proceedings, LXXXIII (Mar. 1947), pp. 273-277. DN
First two chapters of the above entry.

Majuro Naval Air Base

1126. Majuro Naval Air Base 3234...an Informal Record of Life on Majuro in Words and Pictures, 1944-1945. n.p.: 1945. 39 lvs.
Souvenir history.

Saipan Naval Base

1127. U.S. Navy, Saipan Naval Base. "History of U.S. Naval Base, Navy No. 3245." unpublished paper: Admin. Hist. Appen. 38 (16) (I), 15 Oct 1945. 70 pp. DN
Comprehensive history from its early use as a staging area for Pacific invasions to its activities at the end of the war.

Tinian Naval Base

1128. U.S. Navy, Tinian Naval Base, Marianas Islands. "History of the United States Naval Base, Tinian, Marianas Islands." unpublished paper: Admin. Hist. Appen. 38 (16) (G), 11 Oct 1945. 58 pp. DN
History from its organization to the end of the war.

Index
of Authors and Names

References are to Item numbers

Abe, Yasuo, 968, 1024
Abercrombie, USS, 1025
Adams, Henry H., 444, 452
Adamson, Hans Christian, 360, 361
Agnew, James B., 71
Air Intelligence Group, Office Office of the Chief of Naval Operations, 275
Alabama, USS, 957-959
Albion, Robert G, 15, 16, 17
Alcyone, USS, 1028
Allard, Dean C., 46
American Committee on the History of Second World War, 18
Anderson, David A., 276
Anderson, Orvil A., 277
Anderson, Robert E., 1091
Andreieu, d´Albas, Emmanual, 333
Angus, W. Mack, 334
Anthony, USS, 1017
Appleman, Roy E., 670
Army Times, Editors of, 707, 815
Arnold, Archibald V., 611, 820
Arnold, H. H., 429
Arnold, Gen. Henry H., 429-431
Arthur, Robert A., 884
Asprey, Robert B., 499

Bahrenburg, Bruce, 72
Bailey, Seth, 504
Baker, R. W., 985
Baldwin, Hanson, 505, 506
Ballintin, Duncan S., 335
Baltimore, USS, 987
Barker, A. J., 73
Barnard, Roy, 20
Barnes, USS, 923
Bartholomew, John, 1
Barton, R. S., 1080
Bataan, USS, 924

Baylias, Gwyn, 21
Beach, Edward L., 939
Beers, Henry P., 711
Belleau Woods, USS, 925
Belote, James H., 337
Belote, William M., 337
Benis, Frank M., 899
Bennion, USS, 1018
Benson, Douglass L., 650
Bergamini, David, 74
Berger, Carl, 27
Berry, Henry, 75
Best, Herbert, 338
Biloxi, USS, 988
Birdsall, Steve, 759
Birmingham, USS, 989
Bishop, Jim, 478
Bishop, John, 76, 630
Bivins, Harold A., 30
Blair, Clay, Jr., 339
Blakeney, Ben B., 77
Blakeney, Jane, 78
Blankfort, Michael, 434
Blareney, Ben, 495
Blassingame, Wyatt, 278
Bloomberg, Marty, 22
Blount, R. E. Preppy, 794
Boston, USS, 990
Bowers, Peter M., 322, 323
Boyle, James M., 780, 781
Bozung, Jack H, 759
Bridgewater, F. Clay, 859
Brooks, Lester, 78
Brooks, R. M., 1050
Brown, Ernest F., 2
Brown, Richard G., 509
Browne, Courtney, 496
Browner, Charles F., 80
Bruce, Andrews D., 831
Brugioni, Dino A., 510
Bruvold, H. P., 995
Bryan, Joseph, III, 954, 1084
Buchanan, A. R., 279
Buckner, David N., 914
Buell, Thomas B., 448, 488, 658
Bundy, George, 492
Burke, Arleigh A., 432, 469

143

Burke, Vice Adm. Arleigh, 432, 433
Bunker Hill, USS, 926
Burkett, Prentiss, 802
Burne, Alfred H., 81
Burns, Eugene, 511
Burns, James M., 479
Burris, L. D., 906
Burton, Earl, 82
Busch, Noel F., 1112
Butow, Robert C., 497
Byas, Hugh, 83
Bykofsky, Joseph, 84

Caiden, Martin, 280, 313, 316
California, USS, 960-962
Callaway, Raymond R., 920
Camp, Robert, Jr., 1087
Cant, Gilbert, 85
Caporale, Louis G., 638
Carleton, Phillip D., 604
Carlson, Col. Evans F, 434
Carter, Kit C., 282
Carter, Worrall R., 340
Carters, Clyde, Jr., 1001
Casad, Dede W., 471
Cassin Young, USS, 1019
Cate, James L., 283, 284, 760
Cates, Clifton B., 979
Cave, Hugh B., 86
Chamblerlain, John, 463
Champie, Elmore A., 87
Chaplin, John C., 890, 891
Chenango, USS, 927
Chihaya, Masataka, 968, 1024
Christy, Joe, 285
Clark, Joseph J., 435, 659
Clark, Vice Adm. Joseph, 435
Clausen, Walter B., 88
Cleveland, W. M., 786, 787
Cleveland, USS, 991
Cline, Marjorie W., 23
Cochran, Alexander S., Jr., 47, 48
Coffey, Thomas M., 89, 430, 454
Colegrave, E. H. M., 124

Colorado, USS, 963
Columbia Broadcasting System War Corespondents, 90
Collier, Basil, 91, 92
Comet, USS, 1029
Condit, Kenneth W., 93, 94, 900
Conner, Howard, 95
Conner, John, 885
Conolly, Richard M., 712
Constantinides, George C., 24
Controvich, James T., 25, 26
Cook, Charles D., Jr., 96
Cook, Gene, 188
Cooley, Thomas J., 512
Cooper, Norman V., 485
Coox, Alvin D., 126
Corlett, MG Charles H., 436
Cortesi, Lawrence, 782
Costello, John, 97
Cowpens, USS, 928
Crane, Aimee, 98
Craven, Wesley F., 283, 284
Cresswell, John, 99
Cresswell, Mary Ann, 27
Croatley, Robert W., 151
Crossley, R. P., 651
Crowl, Philip A., 142, 639
Crown, John A., 581
Current, Richard N., 491
Cushman, Robert E., 713
Custer, USS, 1030

Danton, J. Periam, 660
Danysh, Romana, 836
Davis, Sumner D., 849
DeChant, John A., 299, 579
del Valle-Barca Munoz, BG Pedro A. J., 437, 714-716
Denfield, D. Colt, 652
Denver, USS, 992
Detroit News, 64
Devine, Robert, 480
Dickson, W. D., 661
Dixon, Joe C., 100
Dod, Karl C., 101
Donahue, Ralph J., 1046

Donnelly, Thomas J., 847
Donovan, James A, 673
Dornbusch, Charles E., 28
Dorris, Donald H., 1014
Dower, John W., 102
Doyen, USS, 1031
Doying, James A., 673-676
Draper, William F., 641
Driskall, Frank A., 471
Dull, Paul S., 341
Dupre, Flint O., 285, 431
Durant, John, 580
Dyer, George C., 498

Earle, Edward M., 103
Ehrhart, Robert C., 138
Ehrman, John, 104
Eiler, Keith E., 501
Ellis, Chris, 342
Ellison, Lee, 791
Emmons, Roger M., 513
English, Richard, 614
Eniwetok, 604-610
Enterprise, USS, 929-932
Erskine, John C., 105
Esposito, Vincent J., 3
Essex, USS, 933, 934
Eustis, Lawrence B., 789
Evans, David C., 343
Ewing, Steve, 929, 943

Faber, Harold, 465
Fabyamic, Thomas A., 106, 287
Fahey, James C., 344
Fahey, James J., 998
Falk, Stanley L., 108, 445
Fane, Francis D., 345
Fanshaw Bay, USS, 935
Farkington, William, 436
Farrell, Don A., 717
Fern, Lee, 758
Fern, Stewart, 758
Ferris, James S., 952
Finch, Percy, 486, 487
Finkelstein, N., 762
Fleisher, Wilfred, 110
Flick, Alvin S., 653
Florance, Charles W., Jr., 111
Forrestal, E. P., 489
Forrestal, James V., 438, 439
Forgy, Howell M., 1000

Fortune, Charles H., 65
Francillon, Rene J., 288, 289
Francis, Anthony A., 718
Frank, Benis M., 49
Franklin, USS, 936
Friedman, Norman, 955, 971
Fuller, John F. C., 112
Funk, Arthur L., 29
Furer, Julius A., 346
Fyre, William, 466, 467

Gabrynowicz, Elizabeth, 832
Gailey, Harry, 719, 824
Galantin, I. J., 1026
Gallagher, Barrett, 347
Gault, Owen, 1092
Geiger, MG Roy S., 440
Genda, Minoru, 348
Giffin, William, 113
Gilbert Islands Operations, 502-576
Glover, Rear Adm. Cato D., 441
Goe, William, 678
Goforth, Pat E., 800
Goodenough, Simon, 4
Goodman, Warren H., 291, 292
Gore, W. B., 720
Gordon, Gary, 114
Graham, A., 679
Graham, Garrett, 515
Graybar, Lloyd J., 115
Great Britain, Admiralty Personal Services Dept., 116
Greenfield, Kent B., 117, 118, 119
Greenspan, Harry, 1021
Gregg, Charles T., 516
Grovenor, Melvin B., 349
Guam, 711-748, 1124, 1125
Guillain, Robert, 120
Gurney, Steve, 763

Haffert, William A., 680
Haley, J. Frederick, 517
Halibut, USS, 1026
Hammel, Eric M., 518, 519, 903
Hammer, David H., 1124, 1125

Handlin, Oscar, 51
Hanecak, R. G., 1080
Hanna, John C., 795
Hannah, Dick, 520
Hanrahan, Gene Z., 121
Hansel, Haywood S., Jr., 293, 294, 764
Hara, Tameichi, 442
Hara, Tomio, 122
Harmon, J. Scott, 1019
Harris, Dixie R., 219
Harrison, John A., 123
Harry Lee, USS, 1032
Hashimoto, Mochitura, 124
Haugland, Vern, 295
Havens, Thomas R. H., 125
Hayashi, Saburo, 126
Hayes, Grace P., 127
Heavy, William F., 128
Heigo, 129
Heinl, Robert D., Jr., 130, 581, 632
Hendryz, Gene, 905
Herald of the Morning, USS, 1033
Herbert, Kevin, 296
Herman, W. A., 1049
Hessler, William H., 350
Heywood L. Edwards, USS, 1020
Hickey, Lawrence J., 796
Higgins, Edward T., 351, 352
Higham, Robin, 52, 53, 54, 55
Hill, Harry W., 582
Hilliard, Jack B., 30, 36
Hilton, Robert M., 681
Hines, E. G., 1011
Hirohito, Emperor, 443
Hockmuth, Bruno A., 682
Hoffman, Carl W., 684, 708
Hoffschmidt, E. J., 217
Hoggart Bay, USS, 937
Holmes, Wilfred J., 132
Hopkins, George E., 297
Hopkins, Harry, 444
Horikoshi, Jiro, 298, 313
Hornet, USS, 938
Hough, Frank O., 133, 193
Howard, Clive, 753
Howarth, Stephen, 353
Howland, Marjuerie S., 59

Hoyt, Edwin P., 134, 354, 355, 541, 642, 1083
Hubler, Richard G., 299
Huie, William B., 135, 136, 137
Hunt, Frazier, 615
Hurley, Alfred F., 138

Ienaga, Saburo, 139
Indiana, USS, 964-967
Ingraham, Reg., 140
International Commission for the Teaching of History, 31
Intrepid, USS, 939-941
Iriye, Akua, 141
Isely, Jeder A., 142
Ito, Masanori, 356, 722

Jablonski, Edward, 300
Jacobs, Bruce, 816
James, D. Clayton, 143, 457
James, David H., 144
Jenkins, Burris, 844
Jenkins, J. C., 915
Jensen, Oliver O., 358, 1113
Joan of Arc, Sister, 472
Johnson, Lucius W., 723
Johnson, Richard W., 881
Johnstone, John H., 93, 898
Jonas, Carl, 522
Jones, Don, 685
Jones, Edgar L., 523
Jones, John K., 433
Jones, William K., 524, 902
Josephy, Alvin S., 886
Jurika, Stephen M., Jr., 477

Kador, Alfred F., 857
Kahn, Ely J., 817
Kantor, Mackinlay, 455
Karig, Walter, 146, 623, 724
Kase, Toshikazu, 147
Katon, Masuo, 148
Kaufman, Millard, 725, 909
Keenan, Richard M., 766, 767
Keesing, Marie M., 149

Kelley, Hubert, 433
Kelley, R. J., 605
Kennett, Lee, 301
Kenney, LTG George C., 445-447
King, Adm.Ernest J., 359, 448-49
Kinkead, E., 686
Kinzey, Bert, 944
Kirkpatrick, Ralph Z., 525
Kline, Edwin H., 726
Koga, Adm. Mineichi, 450
Kondo, Shinji, 32
Konga, IJN, 968
Kroesen, Paul, 813
Kwajalein, 611-620

Ladd, Dean, 526
Land, William G., 654
Lane, John E., 518, 519, 903
Langley, USS, 942
Larkins, William T., 302
Larrabee, Eric, 482
Larson, Harold, 84
Larson, Henry L., 727
Layton, Rear Adm. Edwin T., 451
Leahy, Adm. William D., 452, 453
Leary, R. T., 633
Leckie, Robert, 150
Lee, James, 1100
LeFrancois, Wilfred S., 624
Leighton, Richard, 151
LeMay, GEN Curtis E., 303, 454, 455
Letcher, John S., 887
Lewin, Ronald, 152
Lewis, Charles L., 153
Lexington, USS, 943-946
Lindley, John W., 304
Lindsay, Robert G., 154
Lockwood, Vice Adm. Charles A., 360, 361, 456, 662
Lodge, O. R., 729
Long, Gavin, 458
Lopez, Henry D., 850
Lorber, Donald L., 862
Lory, Hillis, 155
Lott, Arnold S., 362, 957
Louisville, USS, 993

Love, Edmund, 678, 688, 822, 825-827
Lucus, James, 156
Luey, Allen T., 995

MacArthur, GEN. Douglas, 457-463
MacIntyre, Becky, 806
Macintyre, Donald G. F. W., 157, 363
MacIsaac, David, 305
Macmillan, I. E., 634, 730, 731
Madej, W. Victor, 158-161
Mahon, John K., 836
Majuro, 621
Makassar Strait, USS, 947
Makin, 622-629
Manchester, William, 460, 464
Marek, Stephan, 732
Marianas Island Operations, 637-748
Markey, Morris, 934
Markham, George, 162
Marleau, Thomas J., 868
Marlowe, W. H., 626
Marsden, Lawrence A., 1031
Marshall, Chester, 768, 769
Marshall, GEN. George C., 465-468
Marshall Island Operations, 577-636
Marshall, Samuel L. A., 627, 618, 821, 840-843, 846
Marshalls-Gilbert Area, Military Government Section, 584
Martin, Ralph G., 163
Marx, Joseph L., 807
Maryland, USS, 969, 970
Masher, John S., 164
Mason, John T., Jr., 527
Massachusetts, USS, 971-973
Matherson, Daniel M., 165
Mathews, Edward J., 364
Matloff, Maurice, 166, 481
Matt, Paul R., 306
Maurer, Maurer, 167, 749, 750

Maxon, Yale C., 168
Mayer, Sidney L., 169, 461
McClure, Glenn E., 803
McGregor, Carter, 790
McJennett, John, 307
McKay, Ernest A., 308
McKenney, Janice E., 851, 852
McKerracher, Mac, 1072
McKiernan, Patrick L., 528
McMillan, George, 880
Meade, USS, 1021
Meigs, John F., 365
Mercey, Arch A., 170
Merley, David, 66
Mesky, Peter, 1090
Meskill, Johanna M., 171
Metcalf, Clyde H., 172, 530, 585
Metzger, Louis, 744
Meyer, Cord, 607
Miami, USS, 994
Mickle, Peter, 366
Midlam, Don S., 805
Miller, Ben, 919
Miller, Lester L., Jr., 33
Miller, Max, 367, 368
Miller, Norman, 1098
Miller, Thomas G., Jr., 655
Miller, Vernon J., 369
Miller, William, 916
Millett, Allan R., 56
Mingos, Howard, 309
Minneapolis, USS, 995
Mississippi, USS, 974
Mitscher, Vice Adm. Marc, 469, 470
Mobile, USS, 997
Monday, David, 310
Monsarrat, John, 942
Montpelier, USS, 998, 999
Montross, Lynn, 173
Moore, W. Robert, 531, 586, 587
Moorehouse, Clifford P., 588
Moran, John B., 34
Moreel, Ben, 370
Morgan, Henry G., Jr., 174
Morris, Frank D., 691

Morrison, Samuel E., 175, 176, 371, 532, 533, 663
Morrison, Wilbur H., 177, 770
Morrissey, Thomas L., 1088
Morton, Louis, 35, 178-182, 692
Mosley, Leonard, 443
Mourer, Edgar A., 5
Mrozek, Donald J., 54, 55
Mueller, Robert, 282
Murphy, Charles J. V., 311, 771
Musicant, Ivan, 986
Myers, Martin L., 183

Nalty, Bernard C., 184, 185, 534, 589
Nathiel, Richard, 6
Navy Times, Editors, 186
Nelson, F. J., 733
New Jersey, USS, 975
New Orleans, USS, 1000-1002
New York Herald Tribune, 67
New York, Museum of Modern Art, 187
Newall, John, Jr., 1064
Nimitz, Chester W., 372
Nimitz, Adm. Chester W., 372, 471-477
North Carolina, USS, 976-978

O'Connor, Raymond G., 374
O'Neill, James E., 57
O'Quinlivan, Micheal, 36
O'Sheel, Patrick, 188
Okumiyu, Masaatake, 313
Oldfield, Barney, 189
Olds, Robert, 1093
Olson, James C., 754, 755
Organ, F. P., 1074
Ossip, Jerome J., 808

Palmer, Bernard, 788
Palmer, Robert R., 7
Pappas, George S., 37, 38
Parker, William D., 191
Paszek, Lawrence J., 58
Peatross, Oscar T., 628

Pennsylvania, USS, 979, 980
Pensacola, USS, 1003, 1004
Peterson, A. J., 1064
Peyton, Green, 1086
Phillips, W. Dean, 351, 352
Pickeroy, William T., 734
Pierce, Philip N., 192
Pogue, Forrest, 468
Poling, James, 376
Pomoroy, Earl S., 735
Portland, USS, 1005
Posssony, Stefan T., 377
Potter, Elmer B., 378, 379, 473, 474
Poulton, Helen J., 59
Pratt, Fletcher, 193, 314, 380, 475, 490, 537, 591
Pratt, William V., 538, 539, 736
Price, Willard, 194, 643
Proehl, Carl W., 894
Puleston, W. D., 195

Radford, Rear Adm. Arthur W., 477
Rajchmar, Martha, 5
Ravenstein, Charles A., 751
Redditt, James H., 1037
Reed, George A., 196
Reg, Ingraham, 381
Reynolds, Clark G., 382, 383, 384, 435, 956
Rice, W. W., 784
Richards, Benjamin J., 949
Richardson, William, 541
Ringler, Jack K., 901
Ringgold, USS, 1022
Rixey, P. M., 542
Roberts, John, 940
Robson, Robert W., 197, 198
Rogow, Arnold A., 439
Roi-Namur, 630-636
Rolland, Charles, 385
Roosevelt, Franklin D., 478-482
Roscoe, Theodore, 386, 387, 388

Rosignoli, Guido, 199-202, 315
Rowcliff, Gilbert., 738
Russ, Martin, 543
Rust, Kenneth C., 656, 756, 772
Ruth, Joseph B., 912

St. Joseph News-Press, 68
St. Louis, USS, 1006
Saipan, 670-706
Saito, Fred, 316
Sakai, Saburo, 316
Salt Lake City, USS, 1007
Sambito, William J., 922
San Diego, USS, 1008
San Francisco Examiner, 69
San Francisco, USS, 1009, 1010
San Jacinto, USS, 948
San Juan, USS, 1011
Sante Fe, USS, 1012, 1013
Santelli, James S., 904
Saratoga, USS, 949
Saufley, USS, 1023
Sawicki, James A., 837, 853, 858
Schmidt, R. K., 709
Schoun, Karl, 203, 204, 389
Schubert, Paul, 699
Scott, Walter H., 1104
Sears, Stephan W., 390
Shane, Ted, 205
Shaw, Henry I., 546
Shepard, William R., 8
Sherman, Vice Adm. Frederick C., 483
Sherrod, Robert L., 317, 547-551, 644, 645, 693-698
Sherry, Michael S., 318
Shindo, Shorjiro, 298
Shoup, MG David M., 484
Silcox, S. G., 882
Sill, Van Rensselaer, 206
Silversides, USS, 1027
Simmons, Edwin, 207, 552
Simms, Edward J., 319
Sinclair, William B., 773
Smith, Allan E., 664
Smith, Charles R., 908
Smith, Craig B., 739
Smith, Gladdis, 208

Smith, H. E., 740
Smith, Holland M., 486, 487, 700
Smith, LTG Holland M., 485-487, 700
Smith, Julian C., 553
Smith, Myron J., Jr., 39, 40, 960, 970, 980
Smith, S. E., 391
Snell, John L., 209
Snyder, Earl A., 774
South Dakota, USS, 981, 982
Spector, Ronald H., 210, 211
Spier, Henry O., 41
Sprunce, Adm. Raymond A., 488-490
Stafford, Edward P., 931, 1025
Stanley, Roy M., II, 212
Stanton, Shelby L., 213
Stauffer, Alvin P., 214
Steele, Theodore M., 1099
Steichen, Edward, 392, 393, 945
Steinberg, Raphael, 215
Stembridge, Jasper H., 9
Stephenson, Hal W., 394
Stern, Michael, 554
Stimson, Henry L., 491, 492
Stockman, James R., 555, 701
Stott, Frederic A., 910
Streibig, K. C., 1061
Strobridge, Truman R., 907
Stump, Adm. Felix B., 493
Sullivan, W. E., Jr., 320
Sunderland, James F., 321
Swanborough, Gordon, 322, 323

Takeuchi, Akira, 122
Talbot-Booth, E. C., 216
Tantum, William H., 217
Taylor, Rear Adm. Edwin J., Jr., 494
Taylor, Theodore, 470
TeJen, Yu, 218
Tennessee, USS, 983, 984
Thacker, Joel D., 888
Thomas, Gordon, 809

Thomason, John W., III, 896
Thompson, George R., 219
Thompson, Laura, 741
Thompson, Paul W., 220
Thorpe, Donald W., 324, 325
Tinian, 707-710
Togo, Fumihiko, 495
Togo, Shigenori, 495
Tojo, Hideki, 496, 497
Tolbert, Frank X., 558-562, 635
Tolland, John, 221
Travis, Fred R., 742
Trefethan, E. M., 594
Triest, Willard G., 1047
Trumbull, Robert, 1027
Turner, Gordon B., 702
Turner, Jack W., 1051
Turner, Vice Adm. Richmond K., 498
Tweed, George R., 743
Twining, Nathan F., 776

Umezawa, Haruo, 744
U.S. Armed Forces in the Central Pacific Area, 647
U.S. Army Air Forces, 327
U.S. Army Air Forces, Historical Office, 328
U.S. Army, Central Pacific Area, 595
U.S. Army, Central Pacific Base Command, G-4, 563, 596, 629
U.S. Army, Far East Command, 222, 395-398
U.S. Army Forces in the Central Pacific Area, 223
U.S. Army Forces in the Pacific Ocean Area, 224
U.S. Army Forces in the Pacific, G-4, 564
U.S. Army Forces, Middle Pacific Command, 876-878
U.S. Army Military Academy, 228
U.S. Army, Office of Military History, 42, 43, 227, 326

INDEX   151

U.S. Army, Pacific.,
General Headquarters,
225, 226
U.S. Coast Guard, Public
Information Division,
400
U.S. Coast Guard, Public
Relations Division,
401
U.S. Dept. of Army, 703
U.S. Joint Army-Navy
Assessment Committee,
402
U.S. Joint Intelligence
Center, 565-569, 597
U.S. Marine Corps, 897
U.S. Marine Corps,
Historical Branch,
229-232
U.S. National Archives
and Record Service, 60
U.S. Navy, 234, 235
U.S. Navy Bureau of
Medicine and Surgery,
236
U.S. Navy Bureau of Naval
Personnel, 403
U.S. Navy Bureau of Yards
and Docks, 237
U.S. Navy, Central
Pacific, Forward Area,
238-46
U.S. Navy, Commander in
Chief, Pacific Fleet,
404-408, 598-600, 665
U.S. Navy Dept. Library,
62
U.S. Navy, Hydrographic
Office, 10, 11
U.S. Navy, Kwajalein
Naval Base, 619
U.S. Navy, Marianas
Command, 745
U.S. Navy, Naval History
Division, 44, 61, 331,
409-410
U.S. Navy, Office of
Chief of Naval
Operations,
Intelligence Division,
570, 601, 648, 704

U.S. Navy, Office of the
Deputy Operations
(Air), 329
U.S. Navy, Pacific Fleet
411
U.S. Navy, Pacific Fleet
and Pacific Ocean
Area, 330, 412-416,
450, 705, 710, 1102
U.S. Navy, Pacific Fleet
and Pacific Ocean
Area, Communications
Division, 417
U.S. Navy, Pacific Fleet
and Pacific Ocean
Area, Intelligence
Section, 418
U.S. Navy, Pacific Fleet
and Pacific Ocean
Area, Logistics
Division, 419-421
U.S. Navy, Pacific Fleet
and Pacific Ocean
Area, Military
Government, 422
U.S. Navy, Pacific Fleet
and Pacific Ocean
Area, Operations
Division, 423
U.S. Navy, Pacific Fleet
and Pacific Ocean
Area, Public
Information, Office, 424
U.S. Navy, Pacific Fleet
and Pacific Ocean
Area, War Plans
Division, 425
U.S. Navy, Saipan Naval
Base, 127
U.S. Navy, Service Force,
Pacific, 426
U.S. Navy, Tinian Naval
Base, 128
U.S. Stategic Bombing
Survey, 248, 249
U.S. War Dept., 250, 251,
602
U.S. War Dept, Adjutant
General's Office, 252
U.S. War Dept., General
Staff, 12
U.S. War Dept., General
Staff, G-2, 253-57